Hired Guns

Views About Armed Contractors in Operation Iraqi Freedom

Sarah K. Cotton, Ulrich Petersohn, Molly Dunigan, Q Burkhart,

Megan Zander-Cotugno, Edward O'Connell, Michael Webber

Sponsored by the Smith Richardson Foundation

NATIONAL SECURITY RESEARCH DIVISION

The research described in this report was sponsored by the Smith Richardson Foundation and conducted within the International Security and Defense Policy Center of the RAND National Security Research Division (NSRD). NSRD conducts research and analysis for the Office of the Secretary of Defense, the Joint Staff, the Unified Combatant Commands, the defense agencies, the Navy, the Marine Corps, the U.S. Coast Guard, the U.S. Intelligence Community, allied foreign governments, and foundations.

Library of Congress Cataloging-in-Publication Data

Hired guns : views about armed contractors in Operation Iraqi Freedom / Sarah K. Cotton ... [et al.].
    p. cm.
  Includes bibliographical references.
  ISBN 978-0-8330-4982-7 (pbk. : alk. paper)
    1. Postwar reconstruction–Iraq–Evaluation 2. Private military companies–Iraq–Evaluation. 3. Private security services–Iraq–Evaluation 4. Government contractors–Iraq–Evaluation. 5. Contracting out–Iraq–Evaluation. 6. Government contractors–United States–Evaluation. 7. Contracting out–United States–Evaluation. I. Cotton, Sarah K.

  DS79.769.H47 2010
  956.7044'31–dc22

                                                                    2010015412

The RAND Corporation is a nonprofit research organization providing objective analysis and effective solutions that address the challenges facing the public and private sectors around the world. RAND's publications do not necessarily reflect the opinions of its research clients and sponsors.

RAND® is a registered trademark.

Published 2010 by the RAND Corporation
1776 Main Street, P.O. Box 2138, Santa Monica, CA 90407-2138
1200 South Hayes Street, Arlington, VA 22202-5050
4570 Fifth Avenue, Suite 600, Pittsburgh, PA 15213-2665
RAND URL: http://www.rand.org/
To order RAND documents or to obtain additional information, contact
Distribution Services: Telephone: (310) 451-7002;
Fax: (310) 451-6915; Email: order@rand.org

Preface

This research was sponsored by the Smith Richardson Foundation and conducted within the International Security and Defense Policy Center of the RAND National Security Research Division (NSRD). NSRD conducts research and analysis for the Office of the Secretary of Defense, the Joint Staff, the Unified Combatant Commands, the defense agencies, the Navy, the Marine Corps, the U.S. Coast Guard, the U.S. Intelligence Community, allied foreign governments, and foundations.

For more information on RAND's International Security and Defense Policy Center, contact the Director, James Dobbins. He can be reached by email at James_Dobbins@rand.org; by phone at 703-413-1100, extension 5134; or by mail at the RAND Corporation, 1200 South Hayes Street, Arlington, VA 22202. More information about RAND is available at www.rand.org.

Contents

Figures

Tables

Summary

Although a growing body of literature has recently emerged on the topic of the United States' use of armed contractors in Iraq, quantifiable data to evaluate the consequences of using these personnel so extensively have heretofore been in short supply. Our study aims to contribute to filling that gap. Our primary research questions were: What are the costs and benefits of armed private security contractors to the U.S. mission in Iraq, and how have these contractors impacted U.S. military operations in this theater? In assessing this question, the unique contributions of this study are (1) its specific focus on *armed* private security contractors—as opposed to the much larger category of unarmed reconstruction, logistical, and base operations support contractors—and (2) its use of two systematic surveys, one of U.S. military personnel and one of State Department personnel.

The scope of support from armed private security contractors (PSCs) in the Iraq war has been unprecedented. In 2003, approximately 10,000 of these specialized, armed security personnel were providing services in Iraq (Traynor, 2003). By 2004, that number had doubled (Witte, 2005), and over the next three years, it grew to approximately 30,000 (Miller, 2007). By March 2009, this number had again receded to 10,422 (Schwartz, 2009). PSCs work for almost every organization in Iraq. The largest clients by far in the security market in Iraq are the U.S. Departments of Defense and State, and the U.S. Agency for International Development (USAID). However, journalists, reconstruction contractors, nongovernmental organizations (NGOs), and even other U.S. government agencies frequently view them as a logical choice to fill their security needs. Due to the virtual impossibility of surveying military and State Department personnel about only a subset of the private security industry operating in Iraq, the data generated for this study encompass PSCs working for all these groups in Iraq.

What Are the Costs and Benefits of Armed Contractors to the U.S. Mission in Iraq?

With armed security personnel on the ground in Iraq in such unprecedented and visible numbers, they have captured attention both inside and out of the United States and have generated heightened controversy. A host of media and government reports detailing contractor abuses in Operation Iraqi Freedom (OIF) might lead one to believe that PSCs have imposed disproportionate costs on the operation. But other opinions hold that armed PSCs have made vital positive contributions to combat and reconstruction operations during the Iraqi conflict.

Six questions in particular have stirred debate. Three of these take a more negative slant, focusing on the costs PSCs may have imposed:

- Do PSCs have a negative impact on military retention and morale because they are paid more than U.S. military troops?
- Have PSCs had an adverse effect on local Iraqis' perceptions of the entire occupying force because of the legal impunity with which—until January 2009—they operated in Iraq?
- Is there a lack of unit cohesion and systematic coordination between PSCs and the military?

Three other questions assume a more positive angle, concentrating on the beneficial contributions armed contractors may have made:

- Do PSCs play a valuable supportive role to the U.S. military as a force multiplier?
- Do PSCs provide skills and services that the armed forces lack?
- Do PSCs provide vital surge capacity and critical security services that have made the Iraq operation possible?

Our study uses a systematic, empirically based survey of opinions of people on the ground in Iraq to shed light on these questions. To what extent are armed PSCs perceived to be imposing the costs mentioned above? Are any costs that are imposed tempered by positive contributions? In short, how has the use of PSCs affected U.S. military operations in Operation Iraqi Freedom?

Because private military contractors' roles in modern warfare have expanded in the past few decades specifically to augment military forces, we expect that military and Department of State (DoS) personnel perceive armed contractors to be providing military-related services in conflict zones in a way that assists military operations. We therefore set a high threshold of expectations for armed contractor behavior and contributions; any evidence to the contrary in the survey data will be treated throughout the monograph as a cause for concern.

Our Approach

Our study provides important evidence to consider in the policy discussions and public dialogue related to armed PSCs. Focusing specifically on the period in Iraq between 2003 and 2008, this monograph centers on two original surveys—one of U.S. military personnel and the other of U.S. State Department employees, all of whom served in

Operation Iraqi Freedom at some point during this time period. The survey data enabled us to provide a rare quantitative picture of the perspectives of these two groups.

We analyzed our survey results in the context of other data collected for this study:

- **Interviews.** Our interviewees included armed contractors, both active and retired; analysts; trade association representatives; and employees of the Department of Defense, Department of State, and the U.S. Agency for International Development (USAID).
- **Published literature.** Our sources included government reports, memos, newspaper accounts, and scholarly articles.
- **U.S. government purchasing records.**

Do Private Security Contractors Have a Negative Effect on Military Retention and Morale?

The difference in pay between PSCs and troops is a recurring theme in interviews, anecdotal accounts, and analyses of how contractors are affecting the military. Employment with private security firms offers significantly better remuneration than military employment (Spearin, 2006). It also offers a more moderate operational tempo, with better leave options and greater choice of deployment locations. The argument has been made that these more desirable work conditions have the unintended side effect of reducing rates of military retention. However, officials from the private security industry insist that their companies pose no challenge to military retention rates.

Although data on U.S. military continuation rates indicate a fairly steady rate of continuation across the services throughout OIF, our survey data indicate that the prevailing perception among military personnel themselves is that the higher levels of pay earned by armed contractors do indeed adversely affect retention in the services (Figure S.1).

Figure S.1
Department of Defense Survey: Pay

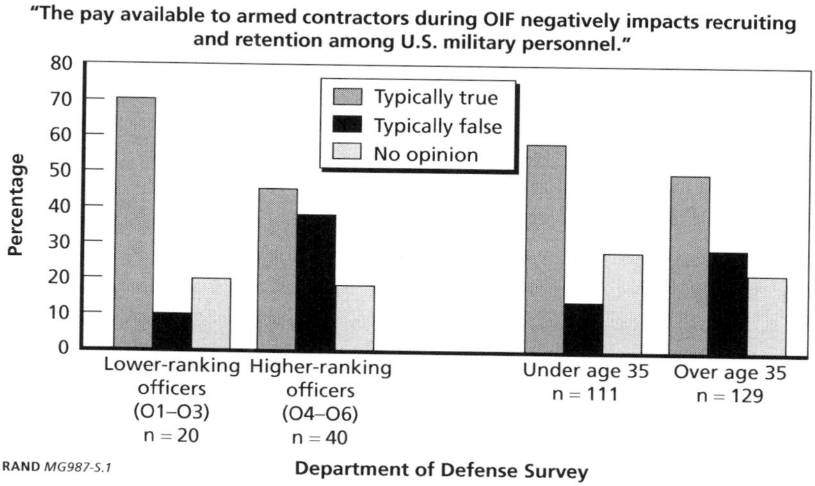

"The pay available to armed contractors during OIF negatively impacts recruiting and retention among U.S. military personnel."

Department of Defense Survey

These perceptions may be deceiving, however: A 2005 Government Accountability Office (GAO) report found military attrition levels within the specialties favored by private security contractors to be about the same in 2005 as they were before the September 11, 2001, terrorist attacks (Lardner, 2006). Furthermore, controlling for length of time in service, some of the retention data indicate that military retention has actually been increasing in recent years. Early-career Army soldiers, for example, are reenlisting in greater numbers: As of December 2008, the retention rate for this group was 20 percentage points higher than in fiscal year 2004 (Milburn and Manning, December 2008). Yet, these issues should all be considered in the broader context of factors affecting retention during recent years. Such factors include military reenlistment bonuses and the possibility that PSC employment opportunities are actually a complementary part of an overall career path for military personnel that could even have a positive impact on recruiting in the long run (Hosek et al, 2004; Hosek and Martorell, 2009).

A majority of the lower-ranking and younger military personnel surveyed also believed that the disparity in pay had been detrimental to morale in their units while they had been in the Iraqi theater.

Have Private Security Contractors Had an Adverse Effect on Local Iraqis' Perceptions of the Entire Occupying Force Because of the Legal Impunity with Which They Operated in Iraq Prior to 2009?

Reports are plentiful of PSCs committing serious, and sometimes fatal, abuses of power in Iraq. The incident in Nisour Square in September 2007, in which armed contractors employed by Blackwater USA killed 17 Iraqis, is the most publicized example. Less extreme, yet still very aggressive, incidents have also been reported.

Our survey results indicate that neither the U.S. military nor DoS personnel appear to perceive PSCs to be "running wild" in Iraq. However, in the experience of military personnel, incidents in which armed contractors behaved in an unnecessarily threatening, arrogant, or belligerent way in Iraq were not entirely uncommon. Although a majority of surveyed personnel had never witnessed an event of this sort, the number of respondents with experience interacting with armed contractors who reported having sometimes observed such behavior (20 percent) is a substantial figure. This is particularly so when considering that we expect armed contractors to behave well when employed in support of a U.S. military mission, even if not employed directly by the United States.

In like manner, although most military personnel had never witnessed armed contractors instigating direct action or taking offensive measures, the fact that 14 percent of those with experience with armed contractors had sometimes witnessed armed contractors taking offensive measures is not insignificant. Similarly, almost half of DoS respondents with experience with armed contractors reported they had never had to manage the consequences of actions by armed contractors (Figure S.2). However, about half of that number had to perform this role sometimes, and slightly less than that rarely had to do it. Considering that having to manage the consequences of armed contractor

Figure S.2
Department of State Survey: Manage Consequences

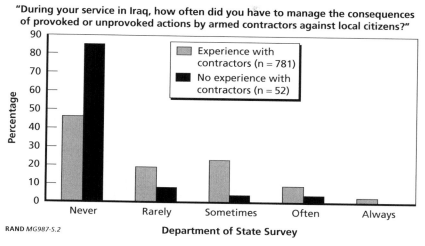

"During your service in Iraq, how often did you have to manage the consequences of provoked or unprovoked actions by armed contractors against local citizens?"

Legend:
- Experience with contractors (n = 781)
- No experience with contractors (n = 52)

Y-axis: Percentage
X-axis: Never, Rarely, Sometimes, Often, Always
Department of State Survey

RAND *MG987-S.2*

actions against locals is entirely outside the purview of what we should expect our deployed diplomatic personnel to spend their time doing, this number is substantial.

These results cast doubt on how frequently armed contractors engage in behavior that would negatively color how Iraqis viewed armed contractors, and thus the occupying force as a whole. Nonetheless, to the extent that Iraqis have a negative view of armed contractors, which can be detrimental to larger U.S. goals in Iraq, such a view is likely derived from a small number of incidents. Hence, the threshold for survey respondents' firsthand knowledge of PSC mistreatment of civilians does not need to be very high for it to be significant. It is therefore troubling that over one-fifth of DoS personnel did report "sometimes" or "often" having firsthand knowledge of armed contractors mistreating civilians (Figure S.3).

Figure S.3
Department of State Survey: Mistreatment

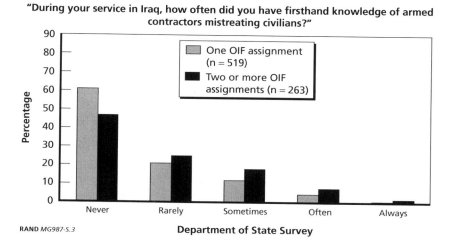

"During your service in Iraq, how often did you have firsthand knowledge of armed contractors mistreating civilians?"

Legend:
- One OIF assignment (n = 519)
- Two or more OIF assignments (n = 263)

Y-axis: Percentage
X-axis: Never, Rarely, Sometimes, Often, Always
Department of State Survey

RAND *MG987-S.3*

Is There a Lack of Unit Cohesion and Systematic Coordination Between Private Security Contractors and the Military?

The ability (or lack thereof) of PSCs to coordinate successfully with U.S. military and coalition forces has been another topic of debate. Two GAO reports from 2005 and 2006 noted several problems in this area, despite efforts to improve. At their extreme, problems of coordination between PSCs and military troops in Iraq have resulted in friendly-fire, or so-called "blue-on-white," incidents.

In light of the numerous reports of failed coordination between armed contractors and the military, the fact that most of the military personnel surveyed had fairly positive views on this issue is surprising. The majority had not witnessed firsthand any failures by PSCs to coordinate with military commanders (Figure S.4). However, among those having experience with armed contractors, the number who had sometimes or rarely had firsthand knowledge of such failures was evenly split at 20 percent each. This is not a negligible figure, considering our high expectations regarding contractor behavior.

A similar majority also had never seen armed contractors getting in the way of active-duty military personnel trying to perform their jobs, but again, 16 percent of those with experience interacting with armed contractors reported having sometimes observed such hindrances of military personnel, and 6 percent of these respondents had often observed such hindrances. Given our high expectations for contractor behavior and contributions, these figures point to the need for improvements in interaction and coordination between PSCs and the military.

Figure S.4
Department of Defense Survey: Failure of Contractors to Coordinate with Military

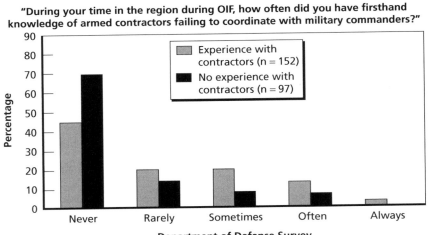

Do Private Security Contractors Play a Valuable Supportive Role to the U.S. Military as a Force Multiplier?

Army Field Manual (FM) 3-100.21 considers contractors, both armed and unarmed, as a valuable means of augmenting capabilities and generating a force multiplier effect (Department of the Army, 1999). Greater support from contractors permits the Army to deploy fewer combat service support personnel and allows the operational commander greater leeway in designing a force. With regard to armed contractors specifically, this school of thought holds that when PSCs provide bodyguards and nonmilitary site and convoy security, they relieve soldiers from having to perform these duties. In this way, employing PSCs generates advantages similar to using unarmed contractors as substitutes for regular troops (Garcia-Perez, 1999; Schreier and Caparini, 2005).

Skeptics, however, hold that the operations of PSCs may inadvertently place additional strain on the armed forces. This is because, when contractors engage the enemy in the course of their work, they may require rapid support from the military.[1] In short, this school of thought holds that PSCs can at times cause more strain than relief for the armed forces, because they may need military aid when under attack. Although such logic applies to both armed and unarmed contractors, the fact that armed contractors have the ability to engage the enemy in a firefight makes this line of thought more applicable to them than to other types of contractors.

In this study, personnel within both the military and the State Department tended to consider PSCs a force multiplier rather than an additional strain on military troops, although such a feeling was much more pronounced among respondents who had direct experience with armed contractors. Two-thirds of the U.S. military and more than half of the DoS personnel surveyed who had experience interacting with armed contractors felt it was typically true that contractors were a means of enabling more combat units to be deployed. Yet, given our high expectations for contractors' contributions to the force, it is surprising that 20 to 30 percent of the entire pool of both military and DoS respondents felt that armed contractors are *not* force multipliers.

However, relatively few military personnel reported having to provide a quick reaction force (QRF) to come to the aid of armed contractors (Figure S.5), with nearly 60 percent of those with experience interacting with armed contractors never having had to do so and over 10 percent sometimes having had to do so. These numbers indicate that instances in which the U.S. military has had to intervene on behalf of PSCs are not the rule, but they clearly need to be considered as part of the cost of relying on armed contractors.

Overall, PSCs are generally viewed as a welcome force multiplier among both military and State Department diplomatic personnel, with troops who have had more contact with them showing the most enthusiasm about their contributions in this area.

---

[1] This strain is in addition to the demands already placed on the armed forces to protect civilian unarmed contractors. A vast amount of military force is needed to provide protection for all civilians working in the theater of operations—at least those under DoD contract (Nelson, 2000; Orsini and Bublitz, 1999; Urey, 2005).

**Figure S.5
Department of Defense Survey: Frequency of Needing to Provide QRFs to
Aid Armed Contractors**

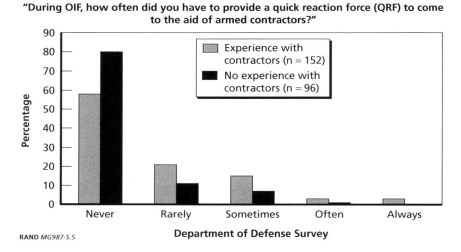

RAND *MG987-S.5*

Do Private Security Contractors Provide Skills and Services That the Armed Forces Lack?

From one standpoint, the employment of PSCs can provide the United States with access to capabilities that would otherwise be unavailable or "would [either] take an inordinate amount of time to develop internally, or . . . be prohibitively expensive to develop" (Wynn, 2004, p. 4). Proponents of this "valuable skills" argument claim that although the vast majority of PSCs provide services that the military itself is designed to perform, a small segment of this group of contractors might be able to offer additional skills.

However, a common objection to the valuable skills argument is that it is far from certain that contractors will actually deliver these high-quality services. Behind this skepticism lies the assumption that because PSCs are profit-driven entities, they may not comply with their contracts if they see a better chance of maximizing profits (Stoeber, 2007).

On the whole, personnel within the military tended to consider PSCs a force multiplier rather than an additional strain on military troops When survey respondents who felt that armed contractors sometimes, often, or always add valuable skills are taken together, a majority deemed the contribution of contractors in this area to be positive.

Both military and State Department respondents held mixed views regarding the contribution of armed contractors to U.S. foreign policy objectives. Two-thirds of DoS respondents said armed contractors had negative and positive contributions, while just over 10 percent felt they made an exclusively positive contribution to U.S. foreign policy. Note, however, that a slightly larger percentage of both experienced and inexperienced DoS respondents viewed armed contractors negatively as opposed to positively on this issue (Figure S.6).

Figure S.6
Department of State Survey: Foreign Policy

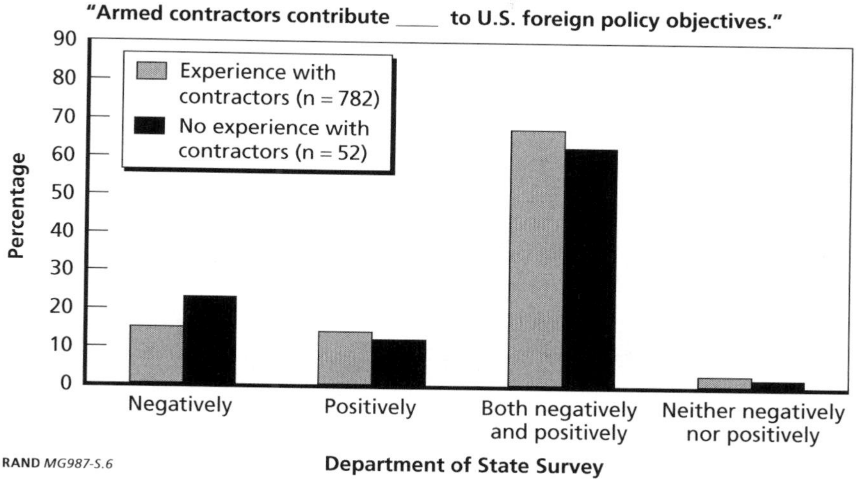

"Armed contractors contribute ____ to U.S. foreign policy objectives."

RAND *MG987-S.6*

In sum, the skill sets and services that PSCs provide to the armed forces are valued by both military and DoS personnel, with the diplomatic group holding those skills in even higher regard than the military personnel. But opinions are much more mixed when viewed in terms of the contribution armed contractors are making to U.S. foreign policy objectives, indicating that anecdotal reports skeptical of the value of armed contractors are not completely unfounded.

Do Private Security Contractors Provide Vital Surge Capacity and Critical Security Services?

For those who take a favorable view of private military contractors, an important contribution is their perceived ability to provide critical surge capacity to the U.S. armed forces (Avant, 2005; Fredland, 2004; Zamparelli, 1999). Although this argument usually refers to contractors who provide logistical support, it has recently also been extended to PSCs.

Opinions that support this viewpoint can be found both inside and outside of government. The Government Accountability Office (GAO), for example, has stated that PSCs are necessary to the Iraq mission, reporting that they fulfill important security functions throughout the country in support of the Department of Defense's military mission and the State Department's diplomatic mission (GAO, 2008).

Nonetheless, skeptics counter that what armed contractors can add to surge capacity is of little value, since their reliability is doubtful:

> The closer contractors are to the battlefield, the more they run the risk of getting in "harm's way." A calculation . . . comparing what the costs of getting into harm are with the costs of withdrawing may actually make it more attractive not to provide a service (Leander, 2006, p. 79).

Figure S.7
Department of Defense Survey: Surge Capacity

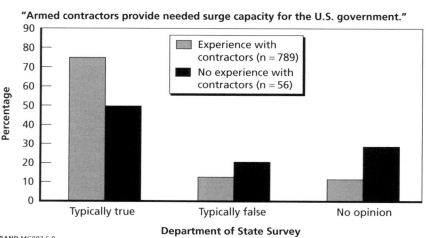

"Armed contractors provide needed surge capacity for the U.S. government."

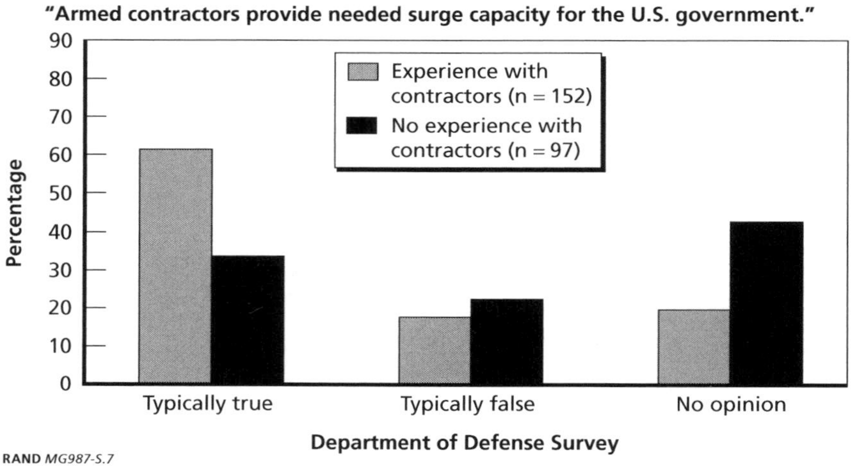

RAND *MG987-S.7*

Armed contractors who directly engage with the enemy are, indeed, often in harm's way and could present costs high enough to warrant careful thought about whether to use them. That said, however, the surveys conducted for this project identified no reliable accounts of armed contractors showing a reluctance to enter insecure areas or to do their jobs when under threat. The central question, in short, is: Have the surge capacity and security services that armed contractors provided in Iraq been an important part of the operation?

Both military and State Department personnel believe strongly that armed contractors provide needed surge capacity. Within the military, a majority held this view, whereas among the diplomatic community, that sense was even stronger (Figures S.7 and S.8).

Figure S.8
Department of State Survey: Surge Capacity

"Armed contractors provide needed surge capacity for the U.S. government."

RAND *MG987-S.8*

Although 18 percent of military respondents with experience with armed contractors felt that they did not provide needed surge capacity for the U.S. government, we are not as concerned about this negative response as we are in some of the other cases, because some of these respondents simply may not have viewed such surge capacity as a necessity.

Summary of Findings and Policy Recommendations

It is clear that U.S. military and DoS personnel perceive PSCs to both impose costs on and provide benefits to the U.S. military mission in Iraq. It is worth emphasizing that the survey data show that increased exposure to PSCs has both a positive and negative effect on one's views of PSCs. Greater levels of interaction with PSCs afforded respondents the opportunity both to witness PSCs' abuses of their position and other negative traits and to gain an appreciation for the positive work that PSCs do. Progress can continue to be made to improve PSC deployment situations if policies are instituted to correct the costs that PSCs impose on military operations, and if other war-zone actors' exposure to them continues to increase over time.

The differences between the perceptions of the State Department and military personnel seem to follow another pattern: the perception of the different roles of PSCs is influenced by the respective needs of the military and the State Department. The military uses PSCs mostly as force multipliers. In other areas, their contributions are not as highly valued.

This is different for the State Department respondents, who found that PSCs were critical for the protection of their personnel and for the provision of organic capabilities not otherwise available in sufficient numbers. Thus, State Department and military personnel tended to welcome the contributions by PSCs more in the areas where they each had special needs that could be met by contractors. However, despite the differences in each group's perception of PSCs, both seem to agree that armed contractors in Iraq have neither a solely negative nor solely beneficial impact on U.S. operations in theater. Indeed, while majorities of both groups of respondents often viewed armed contractors in a relatively positive—or at least benign—light, sizable minorities often reported negative perceptions of armed contractors on a variety of issues. Such minority views should not be overlooked, particularly given our high threshold of expectations for armed contractor contributions to U.S. forces, which, in turn, is based on the U.S. government's rationale for integrating contractors into the force. Whether the costs of hiring PSCs outweigh the benefits is a question open to subjective interpretation that this study does not attempt to answer. However, it is clear that—given the prolific use of armed contractors alongside the U.S. military in modern contingencies—measures aimed at ameliorating the negative impacts of armed contractors would benefit future U.S. military operations.

Acknowledgments

To all of the people who shared their time and thoughts with us during the course of this study, anonymously and not, we owe great thanks. This includes a wide variety of people at all levels from the military and Departments of Defense and State, USAID, trade associations, think tanks, and companies and organizations providing contractors in Iraq. All of your perspectives were helpful to us, and the study would not be what it is without your candid commentary. Thanks are also due to the *Invisible Wounds* project team within RAND, with whom we worked collaboratively during the military survey recruitment phase, and without whom this study's military survey would in the end not have been possible. Moreover, we would like to thank James Dobbins, Michael Lostumbo, Eric Peltz, Chris Paul, Deborah Avant, and Beth Asch for their comments, suggestions, and encouragement throughout various stages in the monograph's development. Finally, a word of special recognition to Thomas E. Stocking, who so ably handled the Herculean coordination necessary to make the State Department survey a reality. While all errors, omissions, and opinions are ours, tremendous credit goes to all of you.

Abbreviations

AR	Army Regulation
CPA	Coalition Provisional Authority
DoD	Department of Defense
DoS	Department of State
FM	Field Manual
FY	fiscal year
GAO	Government Accountability Office
LOGCAP	Logistics Civil Augmentation Program
MEJA	Military Extraterritorial Jurisdiction Act
NGO	nongovernmental organization
OEF	Operation Enduring Freedom
OGA	other governmental agencies
OIF	Operation Iraqi Freedom
OMB	Office of Management and Budget
PIN	personal identification number
PMC	private military contractor
POW	prisoner of war
PSC	private security contractor
PSD	personal security detail
QRF	quick reaction force
ROC	Reconstruction Operations Center
SMTJ	Special Maritime and Territorial Jurisdiction
SOF	special operations forces
SOFA	Status of Forces Agreement
TCN	third-country national

UCMJ	Uniform Code of Military Justice
USAID	U.S. Agency for International Development
U.S.C.	U.S. Code
WPPS	Worldwide Personal Protective Service

CHAPTER ONE

Introduction

What Are the Costs and Benefits of Armed Contractors to the U.S. Mission in Iraq?

With armed security personnel on the ground in Iraq in such unprecedented and visible numbers, they have captured attention both inside and out of the United States and generated heightened controversy. A host of media and government reports detailing contractor abuses in Operation Iraqi Freedom (OIF) might lead one to believe that private security contractors (PSCs) have imposed disproportionate costs on the operation (see, for instance, GAO, 2005, 2006; Westervelt, 2005; Phinney, 2005; Singer, 2004; Associated Press, 2007; Sizemore and Kimberlin, 2006; Committee on Oversight and Government Reform, 2007b; Glanz and Rubin, 2007). The British Parliament's Foreign Affairs committee summed up one of the major concerns with what it terms armed private military contractors (PMCs), which—in the context of this statement— are the same as the armed private security contractors on which this report focuses:[1]

> In undertaking armed combat operations, PMC employees are likely to be placed in dangerous situations, in which the likelihood that they might commit human rights abuses is high. The checks and balances which restrain national armed forces personnel in such circumstances do not apply with such effectiveness to PMCs (Committee on Foreign Affairs, 2002).

---

[1] The literature on private military and security contractors is filled with slight differences in the terminology used to refer to these contractors. This reflects the fact that there are often gray areas between different types of contractors; indeed, one contracting firm providing mainly logistical support services in one theater of operations may expand its services to include armed security in another theater of operations, muddling the distinction between armed security contractors and other military contractors. While the above statement by the British Parliament's Foreign Affairs Committee refers to armed "private military contractors (PMCs)," in general a distinction is made between *armed* private security contractors (PSCs) and the larger category of private military contractors (including logistical, base operations support, reconstruction, and security contractors) of which they are a part. Although this report will focus solely on armed contractors and will use the terms "armed contractor" and "private security contractor" interchangeably, it should be noted that this use of the terminology is not always constant in the literature on these topics.

In contrast, other views hold that armed private security contractors (PSCs) have made vital positive contributions to combat and reconstruction operations during the Iraq conflict.

Six questions in particular have stirred debate. Three of these take a more negative slant, focusing on the costs PSCs might have imposed:

- Do PSCs have a negative impact on military retention and morale because they are paid more than U.S. military troops?
- Have PSCs had an adverse effect on local Iraqis' perceptions of the entire occupying force because of the legal impunity with which—until January 2009—they operated in Iraq?
- Is there a lack of unit cohesion and systematic coordination between PSCs and the military?

Three other questions assume a more positive angle, concentrating on the beneficial contributions armed contractors may have made:

- Do PSCs play a valuable supportive role to the U.S. military as a "force multiplier"?
- Do PSCs provide skills and services that the armed forces lack?
- Do PSCs provide vital surge capacity and critical security services that have made the Iraq operation possible?

Because PSCs' roles in modern warfare have expanded in the past few decades specifically to augment military forces (as detailed in Chapter Two), we would expect contractors performing military-related services in conflict zones to do so in a way that would assist military operations. Therefore, we conducted this analysis with a high threshold of expectations for the behavior and contributions of all military contractors. This high threshold is particularly important for armed private security contractors, because—due to the simple fact that they are, indeed, armed—they have a distinct chance of affecting military operations negatively if they behave in a way that is contrary to U.S. objectives. In accordance with the high threshold of expectations we imposed, we expect that the military and Department of State (DoS) surveys will show that military and DoS personnel perceive PSCs to have had a fairly benign impact on military retention and morale, not to have had any adverse impact on local Iraqis' perceptions of the entire occupying force in Iraq, and to have coordinated well with the U.S. military and coalition forces in Iraq. Furthermore, we expect the surveys to indicate that PSCs play a valuable supportive role to the U.S. military by acting as a force multiplier, by providing skills and services that the armed forces lack, and by providing surge capacity and critical security services that have made Operation Iraqi Freedom possible.

Controversy surrounds all these issues precisely because—in light of the purpose of all military contractors to augment the force—and because of the greater significance of being armed in such situations, reports of armed contractor abuses in the field are so puzzling. To what extent are armed PSCs perceived to be imposing the costs mentioned above? Are any of those costs tempered by PSCs' positive contributions? In short, how has the use of PSCs affected U.S. military operations in Operation Iraqi Freedom?

Our Approach

The privatization of many military, security, and training roles since Operation Desert Storm in 1991 has led to a dramatic rise in the use of armed private security personnel in military and nation-building operations over the past two decades. Often termed "hired guns," these contractors fill critical manpower needs but operate in a murky legal context and do not fit into the military command structure or traditional lines of governmental authority. In the current conflicts in Iraq and Afghanistan, the United States has used them in unprecedented numbers. Private armed security contractors—a subset of private military contractors as a whole—have been deployed in large numbers alongside the military in Operation Iraqi Freedom and Operation Enduring Freedom in Afghanistan. In these operations, the U.S. Defense and State Departments and the U.S. Agency for International Development (USAID) have been the predominant employers of armed contractors, but they also work for journalists, reconstruction contractors, nongovernmental organizations (NGOs), and other U.S. government agencies. This wide-scale deployment is a growing phenomenon suggestive of future trends, with important implications for U.S. military and foreign policy.

Although a growing body of literature has recently emerged on the topic of armed contractors in Iraq, quantifiable data to evaluate the consequences of using these personnel so extensively have heretofore been in short supply. This study aims to contribute to filling that gap. Our primary research question was: What costs and benefits do the use of armed private security contractors impose on the U.S. mission in Iraq, and how does the use of PSCs impact U.S. military operations in this theater? The unique contributions of this study are its specific focus on *armed* private security contractors, as opposed to the much larger category of unarmed logistical and base operations support and reconstruction contractors, and the fact that it draws on two systematic surveys, one of U.S. military personnel and one of State Department personnel.

These surveys contribute important evidence to consider in the debate surrounding private security contractors. Focusing specifically on Operation Iraqi Freedom during the 2003 to 2008 time period, the survey data enabled us to provide a rare quantitative picture of the perspectives of U.S. military and State Department personnel regarding the operations of armed contractors.[2]

---

[2] Note that many of the survey responses are coded to show the distinction between those respondents who had had experience with armed contractors and those who had had little to no such experience. This coding was derived from a question on both surveys asking, "During OIF, how often did you interact with armed contractors hired either directly or indirectly by the U.S. government?" Respondents could answer "never," "rarely," "sometimes," or "often." If they answered "never" or "rarely," they were categorized as "no experience," while answers of "sometimes" or "often" were categorized as "experience."

Survey Instrument Development, Sampling Procedures, and Other Data Sources

After conducting a few dozen interviews over several months with subject matter experts (including armed contractors, analysts, trade association representatives, and employees of the Department of Defense, Department of State, and USAID), we were able to develop hypotheses about armed contractors that we could test with a survey of active-duty military personnel. These conversations yielded a preliminary assessment that the security priorities of armed contractors often conflicted with the counterinsurgency priorities of the military, which conflicted with the nation-building priorities of USAID and DOS. In particular, questions emerged regarding whether the immediate goals of the contractors were at odds with the broader foreign policy objectives of the U.S. government. Anecdotal evidence from these interviews implied that the views as to the usefulness or relative advantage of armed contractors were mixed, at best, which—as noted above—was puzzling in light of the fact the motivation for integrating armed contractors' into U.S. defense policy is premised on their usefulness in augmenting regular military forces. Because our interviews revealed that the perspectives of the Department of Defense (DoD) and DoS were very different, we sought to develop and conduct two separate surveys to compare and contrast the perspectives for employees from these different institutions.

Based on the interviews and aforementioned research, we created a preliminary draft version of a survey instrument for military respondents in September 2006. As we investigated potential sources for a military sample, we identified another RAND project that was targeting a similar population group. (Its final findings are published in *Invisible Wounds of War: Summary and Recommendations for Addressing Psychological and Cognitive Injuries.*[3]) The intent of that survey was to address gaps in the existing literature concerning the prevalence and correlation of mental health conditions and traumatic brain injury stemming from military service in Operation Enduring Freedom (OEF) and/or OIF. Because that study had the advantage of substantially greater resources with which to build a broadly representative sample from scratch (and was designed from the outset to continue as a panel for future surveys related to this particular population), an agreement was reached to stagger our survey to follow that one in time so that we might draw the sample for our survey from those in that sample willing to participate in future research efforts.

The total sample size for our survey of military personnel was n=1,070. This was composed of two sample groups: the original sample (n=953) was drawn from the *Invisible Wounds* study participants based on the following eligibility criteria: time spent deployed in OIF (our study did not include those in the *Invisible Wounds* sample whose deployment experience encompassed OEF only); pay grades equaling E4 to E9, O2 to O6, and all warrant officers; and those who agreed at the conclusion of the

---

[3] *Invisible Wounds of War: Psychological and Cognitive Injuries, Their Consequences, and Services to Assist Recovery,* Terri Tanielian and Lisa H. Jaycox, eds. Santa Monica, Calif.: RAND, MG-720-CCF, 2008.

Invisible Wounds survey to be contacted again for future RAND studies. The second, smaller, sample group was added from the *Invisible Wounds* sample database (n=117) slightly after the initial fielding. This group volunteered for, but was not included in, the *Invisible Wounds* study, because that study did not accept volunteers in its sampling approach. They were "characteristically eligible" for our study as military personnel who served in OIF, however, and were therefore invited to participate in our opinion survey on armed contractors.

After 20 weeks in the field, we collected a total of 249 completed surveys from the military sample (a 23.27 percent response rate.) Because the military sample was drawn from the self-selected subset of the *Invisible Wounds* sample—those who completed the *Invisible Wounds* survey and agreed to possibly be recontacted for future surveys—and because a degree of nonresponse bias cannot be ruled out given that only 23 percent of those invited to participate completed the military version of the survey, its results cannot necessarily be extrapolated to the entire general population of military personnel deployed during OIF.

Given these factors, although it cannot be said that the results of the military survey generalize to the overall population, the authors believe that the greater value lies in the opinions of those people who worked closely with contractors. Therefore, the results of this survey are presented primarily from that subset of respondents. However, it should be noted that, even in cases where the survey question asked respondents whether they had firsthand knowledge of a particular armed contractor behavior or impact, those who classified themselves as not having had direct experience interacting with armed contractors could feasibly respond, because direct experience with armed contractors and firsthand knowledge of incidents involving them are not mutually exclusive.[4] All these observations may now be used to guide further research and can inform more immediate shifts in policies related to the use of armed contractors in situations such as their engagement in OIF.

Because our preliminary assessment indicated that DoD and DoS personnel might have very different perspectives about the roles, benefits, drawbacks, and implications of the widespread use of PSCs, we decided to include a second survey of DoS personnel that could be used in conjunction with the military survey. Permission to develop such a survey in collaboration with the State Department was initially sought in 2006 and granted in 2008. We worked with assistant secretaries in the Bureau of Resource Management and Administration offices, and the Under Secretary for Management, to develop the survey.

The field plan for the State Department sample was much like the field plan for the military sample, but it was condensed into a shorter timeline and benefited from

---

[4] For instance, while deployed to OIF a military respondent could have been in a command post and observed or heard of a problem unfolding due to a failure of coordination between armed contractors and the military, but still have had no direct experience with the armed contractors themselves.

the active support of the survey by the State Department (coordinated through its Diplomatic Security Division). Both the State Department's Under Secretary for Management and the Acting Assistant Secretary for Diplomatic Security endorsed the study. Lastly, the Near East Asia Bureau, which controls the recruitment and deployment of personnel to Iraq, approved distribution of the survey.

The State Department sample was assembled by DoS from the following sources:

- DoS employee list
- Other government agencies (OGA) list (assembled from training records at the Foreign Service Institute)
- 3161s (those with one-year limited Civil Service appointments).

The sample population for this survey was n=1,727. The final State Department instrument contained more than 50 differences from the military version of the instrument. After 33 days in the field, we collected a total of 834 completed surveys (48.29 percent), and 58 partially completed surveys (3.36 percent), the data from which we were still able to utilize. Thus, 892 participants' responses were included in the final dataset (a 51.65 percent response rate).

For more detail on the survey instruments, sampling procedures, and data analysis methods, see the appendixes at the end of this monograph.

We analyzed our survey results in the context of other data collected for this study:

- **Interviews.** Our interviewees included armed contractors, both active and retired; analysts; trade association representatives; and employees of the Department of Defense, Department of State, and USAID.
- **Published literature.** Our sources included government reports, memos, newspaper accounts, and scholarly articles.
- **U.S. government purchasing records.**

Roadmap of the Monograph

Chapter Two provides a brief overview of the history of private military and security contractors, situating the use of armed contractors in Operation Iraqi Freedom within this larger context. Chapter Three addresses the question of whether private security contractors have negatively affected military retention and morale. Chapter Four looks at the extent to which armed contractors have had an adverse effect on local Iraqis' perceptions of the entire occupying force because of the legal impunity with which they operated prior to 2009. Chapter Five considers whether unit cohesion and systematic coordination between private security contractors and the military have been lacking in Iraq. Chapter Six evaluates whether armed contractors have been a valuable force multiplier for the U.S. military during Operation Iraqi Freedom. Chapter Seven addresses whether private security contractors in Iraq have provided skills and services that the armed forces lack. Chapter Eight assesses whether private security contractors have helped make Operation Iraqi Freedom possible by providing vital surge capacity and critical security services. Chapter Nine concludes the monograph with a brief summary of our findings and a set of policy recommendations.

CHAPTER TWO

Private Military and Security Contractors Are Not a New Phenomenon: A Brief History of Military Privatization

As far back as the U.S. Revolutionary and Civil Wars, private contractors have provided support, logistics, and supplies to the U.S. military (Johnson, 2007; Zamparelli, 1999). But in World War II, the practice of using private contractors reached a turning point:

> For the first time in World War II, the manufacturer's technical representative became a prominent feature in forward areas. The increased complexity . . . made the "tech rep" a welcome addition at forward airfields, depots, and repair facilities. In some cases, tech reps were even to be found in the front lines seeking solutions to technical and operational problems regarding equipment supplied by their firms (Charles Shrader, quoted in Johnson, 2007, p. 5).

A directive issued in 1955 by the former Bureau of the Budget encouraging all federal agencies to use private enterprise and civilian business channels for services and goods (Donahue, 1989)[1] set a precedent for the Department of Defense to further expand the role of contractors during the Vietnam War. Contractors were "focused on five major areas: base operations; construction projects; water port and ground transportation operations; petroleum supply; and maintenance and technical support for aviation and high-technology systems" (Friedman, 2002, p. 5). In Vietnam, the use of private military contractors reached a new level, performing a broader range of tasks and deploying in greater numbers within the theater than ever before (Kidwell, 2005).

Prompted by its experience in Vietnam (Nichols, 1996), the U.S. Army issued Army Regulation (AR) 700-137, "Logistics Civil Augmentation Program (LOGCAP)," in 1985. LOGCAP's objective was "to preplan for the use of civilian contractors to perform selected services in wartime to augment Army forces" (Department of the Army,

---

[1] The Office of Management and Budget (OMB), the Bureau of the Budget's successor agency, formalized this policy in its Circular A-76. This circular establishes procedures and policies for federal use of commercial providers (GAO, 2000, p. 5). The Department of Defense (DoD), however, was the government agency making the most use of the circular.

1985, p. 1-1). Five years later, in 1990, the Department of Defense took this initiative one step further, formally making contractors part of the total force:

> DoD Components shall rely on the most effective mix of the Total Force, cost and other factors considered, including Active, Reserve, civilian, host-nation, and contract resources necessary to fulfill assigned peacetime and wartime missions (Department of Defense, Instruction No. 3020.37, 1990, p. 2).

By integrating contractors into the force structure, DoD institutionalized their relationship with the military. As discussed in Chapter One, we impose a high threshold of expectations for armed contractor behavior and contributions to U.S. military operations throughout this study because contractors were originally formally integrated into the U.S. force structure as a means of augmenting the force.

Over the course of the 1990s, the military dramatically expanded its use of contractors. In the early part of the decade, they provided widespread support to both Iraq Operations Desert Shield (1990) and Desert Storm (1991) under President George H.W. Bush. LOGCAP was activated for Operations Restore Hope in Somalia (1992) and Restore Democracy in Haiti (1994) (Nichols, 1996). After President Bill Clinton took office in 1993, he made outsourcing a priority for the armed forces. In 1995, Clinton's Deputy Secretary of Defense, John White, stated:

> The department is committed to ensuring future modernization, maintaining readiness and improving the quality of life of its forces. . . . To meet these pressing requirements, we must find more efficiencies and savings in our internal operations through outsourcing (Gillert, 1996).

The following year, the Defense Science Board, which advises the Department of Defense, estimated the possible cost savings from outsourcing to be between 30 percent and 40 percent (Defense Science Board, 1996). Then, in 1997, Clinton's Secretary of Defense, William Cohen, released his Defense Reform Initiative, which drew heavily on the experiences of business leaders who had restructured and downsized corporations. The principles it laid out—which were meant to guide the transformation of the armed forces so as to enable it to fight in any environment[2]—reflected these insights: (1) adopt modern business practices, (2) streamline organizations to remove redundancy, (3) apply market mechanisms, and (4) reduce excess structures to free resources and focus on core competencies (Cohen, 1997).

At the same time, developments inside the services were creating an amplified need for more contractors. For example, between 1994 and 1997, the Army experimented

---

[2]   As outlined in *Joint Vision 2010* (Joint Chiefs of Staff, 1996).

with digitalized ground forces—the so-called Army XXI. Among the outcomes was an indication that the future Army would rely more on contractors (Hanna, 1997).[3]

By the end of the 1990s, the armed forces were depending on contractors not only to enhance capabilities but also to actually conduct operations (Nichols, 1996; Ezell, 1999). As Gordon Campbell noted in 2000,

> [The] use of contractors to support military operations is no longer a "nice to have." Their support is no longer an adjunct, ad hoc add-on to supplement a capability. Contractor support is an essential, vital part of our force projection capability—and increasing in its importance (Campbell, 2000, p. 1).

When President George W. Bush took office in 2001, his administration launched an outsourcing initiative whose scope went even beyond that of the Clinton administration. The *Quadrennial Defense Review 2001* stated:

> [O]nly those functions that must be performed by DoD should be kept by DoD. Any function that can be provided by the private sector is not a core government function. Traditionally, "core" has been very loosely and imprecisely defined and too often used as a way of protecting existing arrangements (Department of Defense, 2001, p. 53).

In April 2002, the Defense Department's Senior Executive Council launched a department-wide initiative to classify all functions as either core or noncore, with the aim of identifying military jobs that could be transformed into civilian positions. The Army, for example, identified 200,000 positions potentially subject to outsourcing (GAO, 2003b).

Private Military and Security Contractors in Operation Iraqi Freedom

In keeping with this trend, the scope of contractor support in Operation Iraqi Freedom has been unprecedented. In the Balkans during the 1990s, the ratio of U.S. military personnel to armed and unarmed private contractors was roughly 1:1, and the total troops deployed never surpassed 20,000. Before the 2003 invasion of Iraq, *armed* contractors had rarely been used in a war zone. But having believed that "reconstruction would

---

[3]   The constant push toward more outsourcing and the continuous reliance on contractors led to a requirement for more-detailed doctrinal guidance and integration. Consequentially, the armed forces developed their doctrine further to integrate the civilian component. One chapter of Joint Publication 4-0, "Doctrine for Logistic Support of Joint Operations," deals with contractor support (GAO, 2003b; Joint Chiefs of Staff, 1995). The Army, in particular, issued a body of field manuals and regulations dealing with contractor support. The basic policies, responsibilities, and procedures for using contractors on the battlefield were defined in AR 715-9; FM 100-10-2, "Contracting Support on the Battlefield," and FM 3-100.21, "Contractors on the Battlefield," provide more detailed guidance.

take place in an environment with little threat from insurgents or terrorists" (GAO, 2005, p.1), the U.S. government had "made few or no plans for any other condition" (GAO, p. 14). Consequently, when the security situation in Iraq deteriorated, the Army did not have enough troops on the ground to meet the unforeseen demand. This created a serious security gap that quickly broadened the traditional role of contractors into one in which they also provided security. Private armed security contractors were used to fill this gap. These armed contractors worked directly for DoD and DoS, and also as subcontractors to prime contractors, including those who provided logistical or reconstruction services.

The number of armed contractors employed by all entities in OIF grew from approximately 10,000 in 2003 to approximately 20,000 in 2004, ballooning to about 30,000 in 2007 (Traynor, 2003; Witte, 2005; Miller, 2007). By March 2009, this number had again receded to 10,422 (Schwartz, 2009). For comparison's sake, it is interesting to note that during this same period, the number of all types of contractors (armed security contractors as well as unarmed logistical support, reconstruction, and base operations maintenance contractors) was often close to, and at times surpassed, the number of U.S. military personnel in the country. For instance, in July 2007 it was reported that there were 190,000 armed and unarmed private contractors in Iraq, compared with 160,000 U.S. troops (Congressional Budget Office, 2008; Duginski, 2007). By February 2008, this gap had narrowed, with 161,000 armed and unarmed private contractors serving alongside 155,000 U.S. troops (Ivanovich, 2008; Schakowsky, 2007). The ratio of contractors to military had grown again by December 2008, however, when 173,000 armed and unarmed contractors were in the country, compared with 146,000 U.S. troops (Figure 2.1) (Lee, 2008).[4]

Armed PSCs work for almost every organization in Iraq. Journalists, reconstruction contractors, NGOs, and even other U.S. government agencies frequently view them as a logical choice to fill their security needs. But the largest clients in the security market in Iraq are the U.S. Departments of Defense and State, and USAID. Estimates indicate that the United States government spent between $3 and $4 billion directly for private security services between 2003 and 2007 (Congressional Budget Office,

---

[4] Because there are no clear records, it is impossible to measure the exact numbers of contractors and subcontractors employed by all entities in Iraq over the course of the war, particularly during the early years of the conflict. As David Isenberg notes, "For the first three years of Operation Iraqi Freedom, the U.S. government had no accurate count of its contractors" (Isenberg, 2009, p. 8). Therefore, the values represented here for PSCs and for "all other contractors" are approximations, although they are based on various reports and censuses from the field. For instance, we based our estimate of the number of "all other contractors" in OIF in 2005 on John McGrath's calculation that there was a mean of 58,000 non-security contractors operating in Iraq in January 2005 (McGrath, 2006, p. 135). We were unable to find any reliable data on the number of all non-PSC contractors in Iraq in 2003, although the general trend seems to indicate that these forces were steadily increasing during the early years of the war, and tended to outnumber armed contractors. In addition to the sources cited above, this chart is based on figures reported in Brookings Institution, 2003, 2004, 2005, and 2006; Congressional Budget Office, 2005; Merle, 2006; and Elsea, Schwartz, and Nakamura, 2008.

Figure 2.1
Relative Numbers of Armed Contractors, Unarmed Contractors, and U.S. Troops in OIF

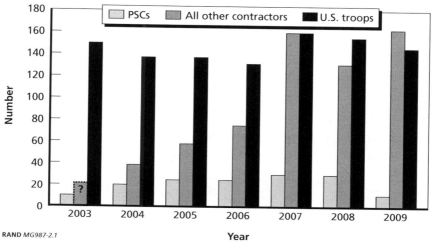

"Number of armed and unarmed contracts in OIF in relation to U.S. troops."

RAND *MG987-2.1*

2008).[5] Of this total, the Defense Department has paid $2.7 billion since 2003 and the State Department, $2.4 billion (Fainaru, 2007c). In addition, the U.S. government spent money indirectly on armed contractors; for example, when PSCs worked as subcontractors to prime contractors. In these cases, the U.S. government was still paying for the PSCs but did not have visibility into their contracts and thus did not have a strict accounting of money spent or numbers of armed contractors hired.

The U.S. military uses private security contractors for a wide range of roles in Operation Iraqi Freedom, including:

- **Static security.** Contractors have been hired to provide security for dozens of U.S. bases throughout Iraq (Fainaru, 2008).
- **Convoy security.** Contractors have generally been used only to guard nonmilitary convoys (Isenberg, 2007).[6] But the Army is running a "pilot program to outsource security on military convoys" as well (Fainaru, 2008, p. 125).
- **Private security detail.** Aegis Defence Services, Ltd., a British firm, protects, for instance, Major General Darryl A. Scott, who is in charge of all military contracting in Iraq (Fainaru, 2008).

---

[5] In this same period, U.S.-funded contractors spent approximately $3 billion to $6 billion for security services (Congressional Budget Office, 2008).

[6] The U.S. military planned to spend up to $450 million in 2007 to protect reconstruction convoys (Fainaru, June 2007).

- **Force protection.** The Army Corps of Engineers contracted with Aegis Defence Services and Erinys Iraq to provide protection (Fainaru, August 2007). In 2007, the Corps renewed the contract with Aegis for $475 million, the largest security contract in Iraq (Klein, 2007).
- **Reconstruction Operations Center (ROC).** Aegis Defence Services operated the center, which coordinated military operations with those of private security contractors in Iraq (Isenberg, 2009).

For the State Department, armed contractors likewise perform a variety of security tasks. Greg Starr, former Deputy Assistant Secretary, Bureau of Diplomatic Security, explained:

> Staffing for security programs in Iraq includes nearly 50 diplomatic security special agents, marine security guards, approximately 1,500 third country national local guards, hundreds of U.S. coalition troops protecting the international zone and regional embassy offices, and nearly 1,500 highly trained contract personal security specialists (Committee on Government Reform, 2006, p. 44).

This last category, "contract personal security specialists," encompassed the private security contractors DynCorp, Blackwater/Xe, and Triple Canopy during the period in question. Security firms working for the State Department are hired under the Worldwide Personal Protective Service (WPPS) contract and perform mainly two duties:[7] First, they protect foreign heads of state. Second, they provide static security for the U.S. embassy facilities and the former Coalition Provisional Authority (CPA) installations (Committee on Government Reform, 2006).

Estimates of the actual number of security firms employing armed contractors in Iraq at any given time over the eight years of the Iraq war vary considerably. In 2005, the Department of Defense calculated that at least 60 firms were providing security in Iraq (GAO, 2005). The director of the Private Security Company Association of Iraq assessed the number to be approximately 181 companies in March 2006 (Isenberg, 2009). In 2008, the *New York Times* claimed that 310 security firms from all over the world had received contracts from U.S. agencies to operate in Iraq (Glanz, 2008).

As of 2008, the Department of Defense directly employed approximately 7,000 personnel to provide security services, while the State Department had almost 3,000 private security contractors under contract at that time (Congressional Budget Office, 2008). The rest of the contractors were hired indirectly, typically as subcontractors who provide security services to prime contractors providing logistical and reconstruction services.

---

[7] Blackwater/Xe has since lost the WPPS contract (O'Harrow, 2009).

Contractors' Legal Status Is Opaque

All U.S. and third-country national (TCN) contractors from 2003 through 2008 were immune from prosecution under Iraqi law under CPA Order 17.[8] However, Article 12 of the Status of Forces Agreement (SOFA) between the Iraqi and U.S. governments, which replaced the expiring United Nations (UN) mandate on January 1, 2009, states, "Iraq shall have the primary right to exercise jurisdiction over United States contractors and United States contractor employees." Interestingly, the SOFA defines contractors as "non-Iraqi persons or legal entities, and their employees, who are citizens of the United States or a third country, and who are in Iraq to supply goods, services, and security in Iraq to or on behalf of the United States Forces under a contract or subcontract with or for the United States Forces" (Article 2, #5). This language would appear to make the SOFA applicable only to contractors working for the DoD, as opposed to DoS, USAID, or other contracting agencies. Yet, because DoS contractors received extensive media attention following the September 2007 Nisour Square incident, DoS officials have stated that they intend to abide by the SOFA and its jurisdictional claim over U.S. and TCN contractors. Other DoS officials have stated that they believe a separate agreement between the DoS and the government of Iraq will be worked out with respect to the legal status of DoS contractors, although it is unclear when such an agreement might be reached (CBS News, 2008).

In addition to the SOFA in Iraq, a number of both international and domestic U.S. laws are arguably applicable to private contractors in war zones, but each has definitional and structural weaknesses that make it difficult to use in prosecuting contractors for war zone abuses. The transnational nature of the industry exacerbates these difficulties because there is currently no standard formula for prosecuting contractors who come from one country, operate in another country, and work for a firm based in a third country. Both the Uniform Code of Military Justice (UCMJ) and the Military Extraterritorial Jurisdiction Act (MEJA) in the United States have been amended in recent years to extend their applicability to war-zone contractors.[9] Furthermore, in

---

[8]   While CPA Order 17 contains language linking its continuation in force to the UN Security Council mandate, several other CPA documents (Order 3, Memorandum 5, and Memorandum 17) set forth provisions allowing for some zone of action beyond self-defense for PSCs. CPA Order 100 extends these measures beyond the life of the CPA, and the U.S. government view is that these measures continue as positive Iraqi law unless and until they are annulled or amended by Iraqi authorities. Thus, contractors may have some legal maneuvering room, even under the SOFA.

[9]   U.S. Senator Lindsay Graham inserted an amendment to the UCMJ into the fiscal year (FY) 2007 National Defense Authorization Act, placing civilian contractors accompanying the armed forces in the field under court-martial jurisdiction during times of contingency operations, in addition to times of declared war. Meanwhile, on May 18, 2004, U.S. Representatives David Price and Martin Meehan sponsored the Contractor Accountability Bill, which would extend the MEJA to include non-U.S. citizens working as contractors to the U.S. government. Section 1088 of the FY 2005 National Defense Authorization Act was then passed in October 2004 to substantially broaden the scope of the MEJA, expanding its applicability to all U.S. government contractors "to the extent their employment relates to supporting the mission of the Department of Defense overseas." Then, in October 2007, the House of Representatives overwhelmingly passed the MEJA Expansion and Enforcement Act

terms of U.S. domestic law, the following are all arguably applicable to PSC personnel: the Anti-Torture Statute (18 U.S. Code (U.S.C.) Section 2340A), which provides for federal criminal trial if the perpetrator is a U.S. citizen or is ever found in the United States; the Genocide Statute (18 U.S.C. Section 1091), which provides for criminal punishment up through the death penalty for a U.S. citizen who engages in or incites genocide anywhere in the world; the Walker Act (18 U.S.C. Section 960), which prohibits U.S.-based financing, initiation, or conduct of military action against any state with which the United States is at peace; the Special Maritime and Territorial Jurisdiction (SMTJ), which extends federal criminal jurisdiction to U.S. nationals on the premises of U.S. diplomatic, consular, or other U.S. missions or entities, or in residences or appurtenant land used for the purposes of these missions or entities; and the War Crimes Act (18 U.S.C. Section 2441), which applies if the victim or perpetrator is a U.S. citizen and covers the crimes of torture, cruel or inhumane treatment (including degrading treatment), murder, mutilation or maiming, intentionally causing serious bodily harm, rape, sexual assault or abuse, and hostage-taking, as well as conspiring to do any of these things ("A New Legal Framework for Military Contractors?").

Reflecting the hesitancy of U.S. prosecutors to get involved in the legal mess surrounding the private security industry, as of February 2010, only one private contractor had been successfully prosecuted under any of these laws: David Passaro, who abused a detainee in Afghanistan, was successfully prosecuted under the SMTJ.[10] The five Blackwater/Xe contractors charged with the 2007 Nisour Square shootings were prosecuted under the MEJA, but, as noted below, the case was dismissed in January 2010 due to tainted evidence. In terms of international legal mechanisms to hold contractors accountable for crimes committed in theater, Article 47.2 of Additional Protocol I of the Geneva Conventions regulates mercenarism in international armed conflicts. However, it does not criminalize mercenary activities; rather, it restricts mercenaries from prisoner-of-war (POW) status, and defines mercenary in a complicated manner, making it implausible for most PSCs to fall under its scope.[11] The so-called mercenary-specific

---

of 2007, which specified that *all* contractors, regardless of the agency for which they provide services, would be subject to prosecution in U.S. courts (Clark, 2008; Isenberg, 2009).

[10] Passaro was convicted on three misdemeanor counts of simple assault and one felony count of assault resulting in bodily injury, and faces a maximum of 11.5 years in prison (Jansen, 2006).

[11] Article 47.2 of Additional Protocol I of the Geneva Conventions defines a *mercenary* as any person who:

    (a) is specially recruited locally and abroad to fight in an armed conflict;

    (b) does, in fact, take a direct part in hostilities;

    (c) is motivated to take part in the hostilities essentially by the desire for private gain and, in fact, is promised by or on behalf of a Party to the conflict material compensation substantially in excess of that promised or paid to combatants of similar rank and functions in the armed forces of that Party;

    (d) is neither a national of a Party to the conflict nor a resident of territory controlled by a Party to the conflict;

    (e) is not a member of the armed forces of a Party to the conflict; and

    (f) has not been sent by a State which is not a Party to the conflict on official duty as a member of its armed forces.

conventions, including the 1976 Draft Luanda Convention, the Organization for African Unity's 1972 Convention for the Elimination of Mercenarism in Africa (OAU Convention), and the International Convention Against the Recruitment, Use, Financing, and Training of Mercenaries (UN Convention), do criminalize mercenary activity, in contrast to Additional Protocol I. However, once again, each defines mercenary in a varied and problematic manner, making their applicability to the modern private military and security industry incredibly unrealistic (Clark, 2008). The fact that one of these—the UN Convention—criminalizes all mercenary activity and yet has never been used to hold PSCs criminally liable for abuses perpetrated in the field highlights the difficulty in prosecuting war-zone contractors using existing international legal instruments.

Another legal instrument with strong potential for holding contractors accountable for their actions (but which thus far has not been utilized in such a manner) is contract law. PSCs are already bound by the terms of their contracts, but most contracts do not include specific behavioral requirements, and even when they do, they are far from standardized across the spectrum of private security firms and activities. Four aspects of the contracting process could effectively be used to regulate contractors' actions: (1) selection criteria; (2) contract-specified obligations; (3) monitoring mechanisms; and (4) sanctions. Criteria for selecting a company for a particular contract could include a requirement that the firm possess all required authorizations, adequate procedures, and standards regarding hiring, training, and vetting of employees, rulebooks and standard operating procedures, internal oversight, compliance and sanctions mechanisms, and/or membership in a reputable trade association and adherence to its code of conduct. Once the contract has been awarded, the contract could include a specific requirement that the company and its employees comply with all applicable domestic and international law. To enforce these requirements, the contract could mandate that the firm monitor and sanction misbehavior itself, through an internal compliance mechanism or otherwise, and should also clearly define the company's reporting obligations. The contract can also provide penalties for breaches of contract, including fines, termination of the contract, and exclusion of the company from future bidding processes (Cottier, 2006). Clearly, the most important factor in applying contract law to PSCs is the manner in which the contracts are written.

All in all, while many laws are arguably applicable to armed contractors, the difficulty and reluctance associated with prosecuting them translated into an environment of impunity for private security contractors in Iraq from 2003 through 2008. During this period, multiple incidents were reported of PSCs firing on Iraqi civilians without cause.

Notably, *each* of these six provisions must be fulfilled for the person in question to qualify as a mercenary ("Protocol Additional to the Geneva Conventions of 12 August 1949," 1979).

CHAPTER THREE

Do Private Security Contractors Have a Negative Impact on Military Retention and Morale?

The difference in pay between private security contractors and troops is a recurring theme in interviews, anecdotal accounts, and analyses of how contractors are affecting the military. Christopher Spearin, for instance, notes that the employment decisions of special operations forces (SOF) are affected mainly by remuneration and operational tempo, and that private sector employment offers both better remuneration and more moderate operational tempo than military employment (Spearin, 2006). In July 2005, former SOF personnel in Iraq were earning approximately $12,000–$13,000 per month. In contrast, some private security contractors were being paid as much as $33,000 per month (GAO, 2005). At the same time, the Global War on Terrorism has only increased the operational tempo for U.S. special forces, which had already seen a threefold increase from 1991 to 1997 in the number of soldiers deployed every week. Employment with private security firms offers a more flexible schedule, with better leave options and greater choice of deployment locations (Spearin, 2006).

Arguments have been made that the comparatively desirable work conditions offered by the private security industry have the unintended side effect of reducing rates of military retention. Because private security firms generally hire only those with at least some former military experience, military retention rates (or continuation rates, as noted below), rather than recruitment rates, can offer some insight into the question of a tug-of-war between the military and private sector over skilled personnel. As Ralph Peters, a retired Army officer and frequent commentator on military issues, suggested in 2007,

> The disgraceful cycle works like this: Contractors hire away military talent. The military finds itself short of skilled workers, so contractors get more contracts. With more money, they hire away more uniformed talent (quoted in Lardner, 2007, p. 3).

A confidential interviewee from the Office of the Secretary of Defense also noted in 2006, "Private military contractors can be a morale deflator for our military guys. They create disincentives for staying with the military."

But officials from the private security industry insist that their companies pose no challenge to military retention rates. They cite a 2005 GAO report that found military attrition levels within the specialties favored by private security contractors to be about the same in 2005 as they were before the September 11, 2001, terrorist attacks (Lardner, 2006). In addition, Doug Brooks, president of the International Peace Operations Association—a trade association representing more than 50 private military and security firms—points out that the vast majority of the armed private security contractors employed in Iraq are not American citizens, and thus the industry's operations in Iraq cannot possibly offer extensive employment opportunities for former U.S. special forces operators (Lardner, 2006).

As noted in Chapter One, we impose a high threshold of expectations for PSC behavior because their purpose as an institutionalized part of the U.S. defense establishment is to augment the force (Department of Defense, 1990). Thus, we do not expect that the survey data will indicate that military and DoS personnel perceive PSCs to have an adverse effect on military retention and morale. This is particularly so because military continuation rates, with a few exceptions, have actually held fairly steady for all the military services over the course of the Iraq war[1] (Figures 3.1 and 3.2).

Figure 3.1
U.S. Military Enlisted Continuation Rates During OIF

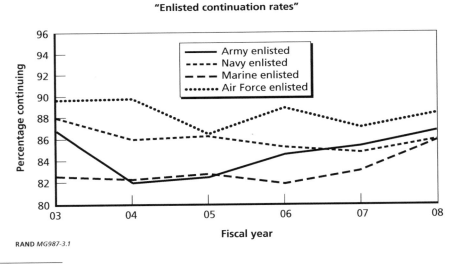

RAND MG987-3.1

---

[1]   Continuation rates are a good measure of retention. Although they do not distinguish between service members in, versus at the end of, a term of service, they do show the overall percentage remaining in service from one year to the next. Note that because the survey asked respondents about military retention in general (and not specifically about retention among the special forces), we looked at continuation rates among the services more generally. Note also that these continuation rates are broken down by service branch to portray the full picture of U.S. military continuation during OIF, even though we do not discuss branch differentiators further in this report. In general, the notion that PSCs have a negative impact on U.S. military retention is not well supported by these numbers.

Figure 3.2
U.S. Military Officer Continuation Rates During OIF

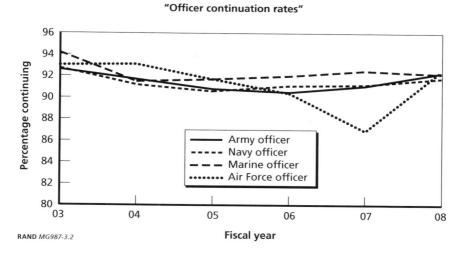

Military and Diplomatic Personnel Tend to View Armed Contractors as Having a Detrimental Impact on Military Retention and Morale

Despite these data on military continuation rates (a good general measure of actual retention), our survey data indicate that the prevailing perception among military personnel themselves is that the higher levels of pay earned by armed contractors do indeed adversely affect retention in the services. Most military respondents felt that this was true, regardless of age or rank (Figure 3.3).

Figure 3.3
Department of Defense Survey: Pay

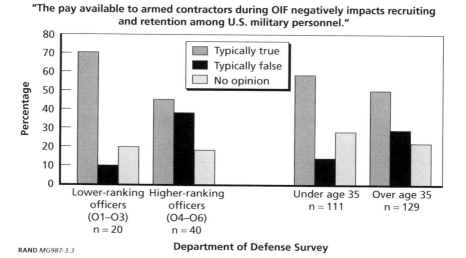

As the figure shows, however, lower-ranking officers and younger military personnel were more likely to perceive a negative impact from the pay disparity than were higher-ranking officers and older personnel: A decisive 70 percent of lower-ranking officers, and nearly 60 percent of younger troops considered this to be true.

When controlling for length of time in service, some of the retention data indicate that military retention (as opposed to continuation) has actually been increasing in recent years. Early-career Army soldiers, for example, are reenlisting in greater numbers: as of December 2008, the retention rate for this group was 20 percentage points higher than in FY 2004. Similarly, in the Navy and Air Force, early- and mid-career sailors and airmen reenlisted at a higher rate in October 2008 than during the same period in 2007 (Milburn and Manning, 2008).

Yet, the relevance of such figures to questions of whether PSCs have a negative impact on retention may be deceiving, as a recent study by James Hosek and Francisco Martorell found that the military has accomplished this increase in retention in recent years largely through the provision of reenlistment bonuses:

> More than any other service, the Army increased the number of occupations eligible for a bonus as well as the dollar amount of bonuses, raising the number of reenlisting soldiers who received a bonus from 15 percent in 2003–2004 to nearly 80 percent in 2005–2007; in that same period, the average value of bonuses increased by more than 50 percent (Hosek and Martorell, 2009, p. 2).

Such bonuses many counteract the negative effects of PSC employment on military retention. Therefore, while these new retention figures for early-career soldiers may foreshadow a growing trend for troops to opt for continued military service rather than departure to a private security firm, recent research on these topics also indicates that maintaining fairly steady retention and continuation rates in the modern era of frequent military deployments will likely come at greater cost to the taxpayer. The effects of PSCs on retention thus have to be considered in the broader context of major factors affecting retention during the period in question.

Another part of this broader context that should be considered when questioning the impact of PSCs on military recruitment and retention is that the services do not desire long careers for their personnel in combat-arms related specialties. The Marine Corps allows only about 25 percent of personnel to reenlist at the end of the first term, as it requires a largely junior force (Hosek et al., 2004). If the situation is assessed in this light, the availability of PSC employment opportunities could be viewed as a complementary part of an overall career pattern in which people join the military, serve for one or several terms, and then enter the private sector to work for a PSC. According to this view, one might make the argument that PSC positions have a positive effect on recruiting and enable the military to attract more people into the combat arms specialties than would otherwise be the case. While our research did not explore this possibility directly, it poses an interesting issue for future research. Therefore, while the option

Figure 3.4
Department of Defense Survey: Morale

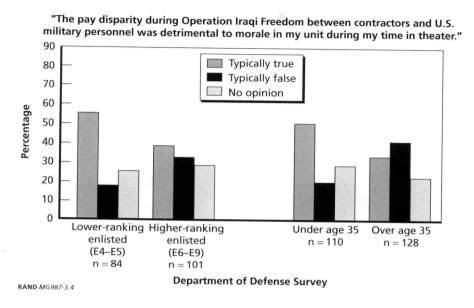

"The pay disparity during Operation Iraqi Freedom between contractors and U.S. military personnel was detrimental to morale in my unit during my time in theater."

of PSC employment may affect military retention at the margin, the broader context in which such retention effects occur should not be overlooked.

The question of morale is closely related to the debate about the effect of higher contractor salaries on retention. Should the pay disparity between private security contractors and members of the armed forces dampen military morale, this could fuel the argument that higher contractor pay has a negative effect on retention, because lower morale would understandably be a disincentive to reenlist.

The military personnel surveyed—all of whom had served in Iraq—did believe that the disparity in pay had been detrimental to morale in their units while they had been in the Iraqi theater (Figure 3.4). Again, this was the majority view regardless of age or rank. But more lower-ranking and younger military personnel were of this opinion than their higher-ranking and older counterparts. The fact that older and higher-ranking military personnel seem less bothered by the pay disparity with private security contractors suggests that one's own financial situation and, possibly, comfort with career decisions over a longer time horizon, may play a role in shaping perceptions on this issue.

Viewing the issue from outside the military, State Department personnel in our survey largely seconded the general perception within the armed forces. The majority of lower-earning diplomatic personnel and those younger than 35 felt that during the time they were posted to Iraq, the relatively higher pay of armed contractors had a clearly detrimental effect on U.S. military morale (Figure 3.5). However, fewer higher earners than lower earners felt the higher contractor pay had a negative effect, and

Figure 3.5
Department of State Survey: Pay Disparity

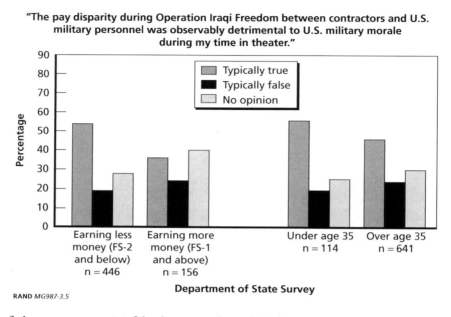

"The pay disparity during Operation Iraqi Freedom between contractors and U.S. military personnel was observably detrimental to U.S. military morale during my time in theater."

RAND *MG987-3.5*

fewer of those over age 35 felt this way than did their younger counterparts. Again, these results indicate that one's financial situation and age might shape views in this area, with older, more financially secure individuals being less troubled by contractors' relatively higher pay.

CHAPTER FOUR

Have Private Security Contractors Had an Adverse Effect on Local Iraqis' Perceptions of the Entire Occupying Force Because of the Legal Impunity with Which They Operated in Iraq Prior to 2009?

As noted in Chapter Two, the legal status of contractors in Iraq was altered significantly in 2009. Article 12 of the Status of Forces Agreement (SOFA) between the Iraqi and U.S. governments, which replaced the expiring UN mandate on January 1, 2009, states, "Iraq shall have the primary right to exercise jurisdiction over United States contractors and United States contractor employees." This removed the legal immunity that U.S. and third-country national (TCN) contractors had enjoyed in Iraq from 2003 through 2008 under CPA Order 17. While the language of the SOFA appears to make it applicable only to contractors working for the DoD, as opposed to DoS, USAID, or other contracting agencies, DoS officials have stated that they intend to abide by the SOFA and its jurisdictional claim over U.S. and TCN contractors. Other DoS officials have stated that they believe a separate agreement between the DoS and the government of Iraq will be worked out with respect to the legal status of DoS contractors, although it is unclear when such an agreement might be reached (CBS News, 2008).

Even with the SOFA's entry into force, however, PSCs are generally thought to be effectively immune from prosecution under U.S. law, as discussed in detail in Chapter Two. The legal void in which private security contractors in Iraq had operated until the SOFA entered into force in 2009 had a bearing on local Iraqis' perceptions of contractors and their activities. Some have argued that these perceptions have colored locals' views of coalition operations in general.

Confirmed Incidents of Armed Contractors Firing on Iraqi Civilians

Reports are plentiful of private security contractors committing serious, sometimes fatal, abuses of power in Iraq. Consider, for instance, the highly publicized September 2007 Nisour Square incident, in which a team of contractors working for the company known at that time as Blackwater (now called Xe Services) providing personal security details for State Department officials stopped traffic in a busy Baghdad square and proceeded to shoot and kill 17 civilians, wounding numerous others (Glanz and Rubin, 2007a, 2007b; Oppel and Gordon, 2007; Johnston and Broder, 2007; Logan, 2007). Conflicting reports exist regarding whether the Blackwater/Xe contractors came under hostile fire and were acting in self-defense. The Blackwater/Xe guards said they believed that they had come under small-arms fire from insurgents, so they began firing machine guns, grenade launchers, and a sniper rifle in Nisour Square. But investigators concluded that the guards had indiscriminately fired in an unprovoked assault (Williams, 2010). The fact that these contractors were immune to prosecution under Iraqi law meant that months went by before they were indicted in the United States under the MEJA.

In another documented case from 2006, contractors working for Triple Canopy in Iraq shot and killed civilians for no apparent reason other than "for sport" (Fainaru, 2007a, p. A01). Unlike contractors involved in the more highly publicized Blackwater/Xe case, these Triple Canopy personnel completely escaped prosecution.

Brigadier General Karl Horst, deputy commander of the U.S. Army's 3rd Infantry Division, identified this problem even earlier. He counted twelve shootings and at least six Iraqi civilian deaths within two months in 2005. As General Horst put it,

> These guys [i.e., armed contractors] run loose in this country and do stupid stuff. There's no authority over them, so you can't come down on them hard when they escalate force. They shoot people, and someone else has to deal with the aftermath (quoted in Singer, 2007, p. 8).

There is evidence that such alleged abuses of power by private security contractors, carried out with impunity, have influenced local Iraqis' perceptions of contractors and their activities and, arguably, of coalition operations in general. Extrapolating from their experiences with private security contractors, Iraqi citizens may take a negative view of the entire military occupation and coalition forces as a whole. But another perspective on this issue does exist. Other accounts hold that at least some private security firms have been flexible enough in their standard operating procedures to keep a low profile among local civilians and therefore have not colored Iraqi opinion negatively.

Interviews with family members of the Nisour Square victims indicate that they and other Iraqis resent both the contractors themselves and Blackwater/Xe as a whole. The incident fueled the perception among Iraqis more broadly that U.S. private security contractors can act with impunity. This engendered widespread resentment and led the Iraqi government to vow that the perpetrators of the Nisour Square deaths in Baghdad would be tried in Iraqi courts (Luban, 2007). Such resentment was exacerbated among both Iraqi civilians and government officials when, on December 31, 2009, Justice Ricardo M. Urbina dismissed the manslaughter and weapons charges against the Blackwater/Xe contractors involved in the Nisour Square incident, ruling that the U.S. Justice Department's investigation had been badly tainted by statements the guards provided to the State Department under promises of immunity. In late January 2010, the U.S. government appealed this ruling, and the Iraqi government started collecting signatures for a class-action lawsuit from victims who were wounded or lost family members in incidents involving Blackwater/ Xe ("U.S. Appeals Ruling in Blackwater Case," 2010; "Iraq to Seek Compensation for Contractor Incidents," 2010).

Although Nisour Square and the incident involving the Triple Canopy contractors were two unusually extreme cases of the alleged abuse of power by private security contractors, less extreme instances have also been reported. Accounts maintain that some armed contractors, when conducting private security details, employ aggressive tactics to ward off potential attackers—for example, driving on the wrong side of the road and firing warning shots (Singer, 2007). Similar accounts describe contractors forcing Iraqis off the road while driving fast and recklessly. Armed contractors have also reportedly cleared areas by throwing full water bottles at local civilians while driving through (Montagne and Temple-Raston, 2007).

Retired U.S. Marine Colonel Thomas X. Hammes has argued that Blackwater/ Xe's aggressive approach to protection has detracted from the overall counterinsurgency effort to win the allegiance of the local population:

> The problem is [that] in protecting the principal, they had to be very aggressive, and each time they went out they had to offend locals, forcing them to the side of the road, being overpowering and intimidating, at times running vehicles off the road, making enemies each time they went out (quoted in Luban, 2007, p. 1).

Blackwater/Xe has received the majority of such criticism. But employees of other security firms have reportedly acted in similar ways both in Iraq and other theaters. A USAID official with experience in Afghanistan noted in a 2006 interview:

> DynCorp, Kroll, Global, and their operations are in Afghanistan. The way that they behave in public is quite offensive by any standard. In a small town, they drive quickly; shooters shoot at traffic; they force their cars through. That is not only when they are escorting the Ambassador. It is also when they are just driving around town or to the airport. I questioned them on a number of occasions. They think that it is harder for a suicide bomber to kill you if you are driving very quickly and weaving through traffic. So they think of it as a safety precaution. It's not clear to me that this is true. This is an excellent example of misplacing our priorities . . . They exhibit a level of arrogance that is just difficult to describe unless you actually view it. . . . Fear is contrary to our interest. In the last four years, people have been forced to flee for their lives in the face of U.S. security vehicles. It is not the military that drives like that . . . there have been hundreds of times that I've seen PMCs do it. They behave in public in a threatening manner. It is part of their rules of engagement. Many of the shooters were decent guys. At the same time, as of July 2005, these kinds of intimidating incidents happened all the time (confidential interview, 2006).

The damage done by such alleged abuses of power by private security contractors, carried out with impunity, reportedly goes far beyond merely fostering a dim view among Iraqis of the contractors themselves. Extrapolating from their experiences with private security contractors, Iraqi citizens may take a negative view of the entire military occupation and coalition forces as a whole. According to media reports and interviews, resentment occurs mainly because Iraqi civilians do not distinguish between private contractors and U.S. or coalition forces in Iraq. Rather, they see them all as part of the same occupying force (Montagne and Temple-Raston, 2007). With regard specifically to the Nisour Square shooting, a National Public Radio report observed the following:

> The more immediate concern is that Blackwater's actions in Iraq don't just reflect on the security company. It has become a broader American problem because Iraqis don't distinguish between the Blackwater employees and the American military more generally (Montagne and Temple-Raston, 2007).

When asked if he had learned who perpetrated the Nisour Square shootings after the fact, a family member of two of the Nisour Square victims answered, "You mean, like, security company? What difference this makes? They are Americans" (Montagne and Temple-Raston, 2007).

However, another perspective on the conduct of armed contractors does exist. According to a group of USAID interviewees, although more the exception than the rule, certain private security firms were able to be flexible in their standard operating procedures and keep a "low profile" among local civilians:

> We hired Kroll, from a British base. They were former SAS guys. Other than some management problems, overall they did a pretty good—an excellent job . . . They learned how to keep a low profile. Now these other guys: Triple Canopy, Blackwater, etc.? They don't change their tactics . . . Kroll learned how to work with us. They were more controllable. [Their] guys on the ground did well . . . With Kroll it was not a problem. They kept guns in the car. It was very nonimposing (confidential interview, 2006).

Most Military and Diplomatic Personnel Do Not View Armed Contractors as "Running Wild" in Iraq, but a Considerable Number of Both Groups Do Report Troubling Incidents Involving Poor PSC Behavior Toward Iraqi Civilians

As noted in Chapter One, throughout this study we have imposed a high threshold of expectations for the behavior of armed contractors. This is due to the fact that their institutionalized position in the U.S. defense establishment is premised on their purpose of augmenting the force. Therefore, with regard to their impact on local civilians in the theater in which they operate, particularly when they serve as part of a counterinsurgency force, we expect that military and diplomatic survey respondents will

Figure 4.1
Department of Defense Survey: Threatening Action

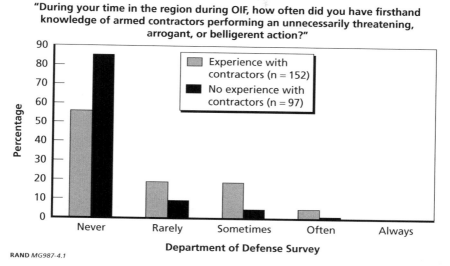

RAND *MG987-4.1*

perceive PSC behavior to be positive. Any evidence to the contrary, although presaged in reports such as those highlighting the Nisour Square incident, is a cause for concern.

In the experience of military personnel, incidents in which armed contractors behaved in an unnecessarily threatening, arrogant, or belligerent way in Iraq were not entirely uncommon. Although the majority of surveyed personnel had never witnessed an event of this sort, the numbers become much more striking when we control for those respondents who had experience with armed contractors. Although a majority of these respondents with contractor experience still reported never having witnessed armed contractors behaving in an unnecessarily threatening, arrogant, or belligerent manner in Iraq, the number of experienced respondents who reported having sometimes observed such behavior (20 percent of those with experience interacting with armed contractors) is a substantial figure, as is the number reporting having often observed such behavior (almost 5 percent; see Figure 4.1). This is particularly so when considering that we expect armed contractors to behave well when employed in support of a U.S. military mission, even if they are not employed directly by the United States.

In like manner, most military personnel had never witnessed armed contractors instigating direct action or taking offensive measures unprovoked (Figure 4.2). Again, it makes sense that this would be the case among the group with little to no exposure to contractors; however, even among those who did have experience with contractors, 65 percent had never witnessed this occurring. Yet, once again, the fact that 14 percent of this experienced group had sometimes witnessed armed contractors taking offensive measures unprovoked and almost 5 percent had often witnessed this happening, is not insignificant.

Figure 4.2
Department of Defense Survey: Unprovoked Action

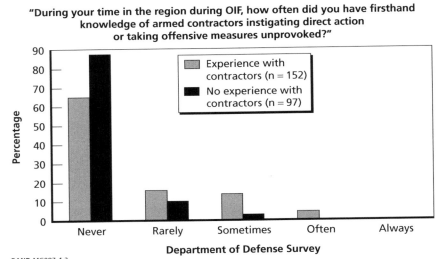

"During your time in the region during OIF, how often did you have firsthand knowledge of armed contractors instigating direct action or taking offensive measures unprovoked?"

Department of Defense Survey

The opinions of State Department personnel add another valuable perspective to the military insights when considering the debate around the behavior of private security contractors and its potential effect on how Iraqis view the occupying force. Almost 50 percent of diplomatic personnel with experience interacting with armed contractors did not think, for example, that armed contractors demonstrate an understanding and sensitivity to Iraqis and their culture (Figure 4.3).

When it came to the issue of contractors' respect for local and international laws, opinions among diplomatic personnel who had interacted with contractors were split

Figure 4.3
Department of State Survey: Sensitivity

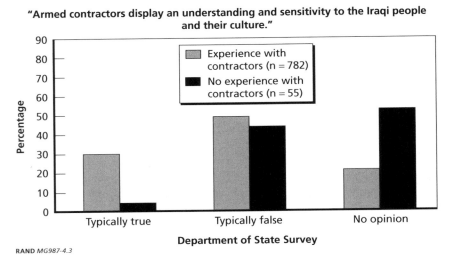

"Armed contractors display an understanding and sensitivity to the Iraqi people and their culture."

Department of State Survey

Figure 4.4
Department of State Survey: Respectful

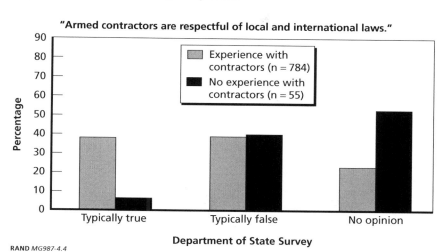

RAND *MG987-4.4*

between those thinking that armed contractors do respect local and international laws and those thinking that they do not (38 percent and 39 percent, respectively; Figure 4.4).[1] The fact that a slightly higher percentage of DoS survey respondents felt that armed contractors are not respectful of local and international laws than those that did feel PSCs are respectful of such laws is a cause for deep concern, particularly in light of the counterinsurgency mission of the United States in Iraq and the possibility highlighted above that Iraqi civilians do not distinguish between coalition forces and armed contractors. In such a counterinsurgency situation, U.S forces do not want to be perceived as being disrespectful of Iraqi and international laws; yet contractor actions bring such perceptions into the realm of possibility.

A majority of State Department personnel who had been deployed to OIF once had also never had firsthand knowledge of armed contractors mistreating Iraqi civilians (Figure 4.5). However, in light of the fact that we would never expect PSCs to mistreat Iraqi civilians, the number of DoS respondents who sometimes had firsthand knowledge of such incidents is, again, a cause for concern. Interestingly, the likelihood increased with the number of postings a person had had: Of those with only one assignment to Iraq, 61 percent never and 12 percent sometimes knew firsthand about armed contractors mistreating civilians; of those with two or more assignments, 47 percent never and 18 percent sometimes had such knowledge.

---

[1] The opinions of diplomatic personnel did suggest that armed contractors were making some progress over time on this issue. Of those diplomats who had been assigned once to the region between 2001 and 2006, only 29 percent felt armed contractors respected local and international laws. But among those with a single assignment to the region later in the conflict, between 2007 and 2008, the percentage holding this view had increased considerably, to 40 percent.

Figure 4.5
Department of State Survey: Mistreatment

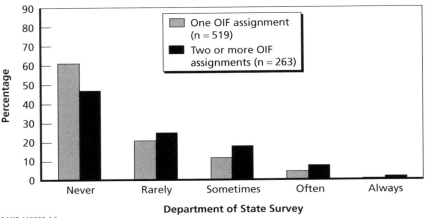

"During your service in Iraq, how often did you have firsthand knowledge of armed contractors mistreating civilians?"

RAND *MG987-4.5*

With regard to the question of whether they perceived armed contractors to enjoy free reign to misbehave with little accountability, DoS respondents' levels of experience with PSCs appear to play a decisive role. Nearly two-thirds of the experienced group felt that such a contention was false (Figure 4.6). Interestingly, however, their counterparts with little to no experience had a dramatically different view, with only about 18 percent believing it to be false, and 32 percent feeling that contractor accountability was lacking. This gap suggests that increased exposure to private security contractors over time causes awareness in the diplomatic community that these armed personnel are actually more accountable for their actions than one might initially think.

Figure 4.6
Department of State Survey: Free Reign

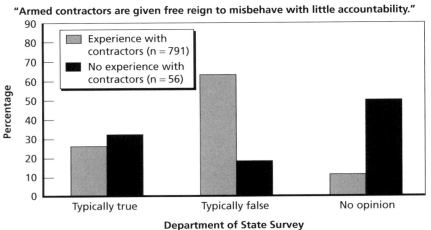

"Armed contractors are given free reign to misbehave with little accountability."

RAND *MG987-4.6*

Yet despite the mix of positive and negative views within the State Department on armed contractors and how they interact with Iraqi civilians, diplomatic personnel rarely had to manage any consequences of provoked or unprovoked action against local citizens (Figure 4.7). Those without experience with contractors would logically not report having had to do this, because less exposure would afford fewer opportunities to manage the consequences of any untoward actions. And indeed, nearly 90 percent had never been in this situation. But, of those State Department personnel posted to Iraq who had experience with armed contractors, almost half had never been called on in this way. As Figure 4.7 shows, about half of that number had to perform this role sometimes, and slightly less than that rarely had to do it. However, we must consider that having to manage the consequences of armed contractor actions against locals is entirely outside of the purview of what we should expect our deployed diplomatic personnel to spend their time doing. This is because, again, the entire purpose of private military and security contractors is to augment the force, not to detract from it or challenge it. In light of this, it is striking that 9 percent of DoS respondents with experience with armed contractors reported often having to manage the consequences of armed contractor actions.

All in all, it does not appear that a majority of either the military or State Department personnel perceive private security contractors to be "running wild" in Iraq. But there are significant and disconcerting indicators in the survey data that the military and diplomatic communities feel there might be a basis—at least in the attitudes that armed contractors bring to the country—for Iraqis to take a dim view of them, consequently damaging the standing of coalition forces in general among the local populace. Greater exposure to contractors over a longer span of time also seems to provide a more

Figure 4.7
Department of State Survey: Manage Consequences

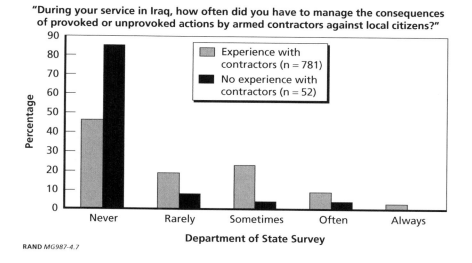

"During your service in Iraq, how often did you have to manage the consequences of provoked or unprovoked actions by armed contractors against local citizens?"

Legend: Experience with contractors (n = 781); No experience with contractors (n = 52)

Department of State Survey

negative view of how contractors do indeed conduct themselves with regard to civilians in Iraq, while simultaneously providing a more positive view of the degree to which they are actually accountable for their actions.

Reforms Appear to Have Had a Positive Impact Thus Far

After the Nisour Square incident in September 2007, the Departments of Defense and State undertook steps to improve oversight over PSCs. Immediately after the incident, Secretary of Defense Robert Gates pressed all military commanders to investigate and pursue any wrongdoing by contractors (Department of Defense, 2007). In October 2007, the Pentagon announced that the military would improve oversight over coordination, movement, and training of the numerous armed parties in theater. The State Department also initiated new oversight measures. Cameras are now required in PSC vehicles, transmissions are to be recorded, and State Department personnel are embedded with personal security details (PSDs) (Broder and Johnston, 2007). On December 5, 2007, the State and Defense Departments signed a Memorandum of Agreement that defined areas of responsibility, required the establishment of coordination mechanisms, and provided tightened rules for the use of force (Department of Defense and Department of State, 2007). Survey results indicate that 75 percent of the State Department personnel who were in Iraq from 2007 through 2008 were aware of the reforms, indicating that the State Department successfully informed its employees about these measures.

There are several reasons to be skeptical about whether these measures will make a difference. First, the military had addressed the coordination problem long before the Nisour Square incident. The Reconstruction Operations Center had been established in 2004 to enhance coordination between the military and contractors. Second, even if the military intends to ensure a high training standard for contractors, there is some question as to whether this would significantly change contractor behavior. The required training standards under the WPPS contract are among the highest in the industry, and the Blackwater/Xe contractors involved in the Nisour Square incident had all been trained accordingly. Third, the State Department's plan of embedding its own personnel in the convoys to increase oversight is also unlikely to make a difference. State Department personnel were already in control of contractor oversight prior to the Nisour Square incident, and the addition of personnel to convoys is not intended to place them in command or to furnish them with enhanced legal powers for prosecution. Fourth, many vehicles had already been equipped with cameras before the incident (Isenberg, 2009). There is no guarantee that the cameras will catch incidents or all necessary information, since they usually cover only the front view. Fifth, rules for the use of force were strict prior to the Nisour Square incident. Force was only allowed in self-defense and the contractors had to comply with strict procedures pertaining to the escalation of force. Nonetheless, some firms gained a reputation of being trigger happy (Broder and Johnston, 2007).

In spite of the low probability that these reforms would be effective, the GAO was slightly more positive about the impact of the new regulations:

> Since that incident, DoD and the State Department have taken steps to increase oversight and coordination over PSCs. . . . The improvements DoD and the State Department have made may reduce the number of PSC incidents in Iraq. However, these enhancements may not eliminate incidents. Moreover, while the increase in the number of DoD personnel devoted to PSC oversight in Iraq should improve oversight, more efforts are required to ensure that that these personnel are well-trained and qualified, and that positions are filled and sustained over time (GAO, 2008, p. 30).

Furthermore, the 2009 Commission on Wartime Contracting in Iraq and Afghanistan's Interim Report, *At What Cost: Contingency Contracting in Iraq and Afghanistan,* noted a significant decline in "WPPS use of deadly force incidents" between 2007 and 2009, attributing the improvement to the new policies that had been enacted:

> Many congressional and agency process improvements in the management of personal security contracts appear to have led to a decrease in incidents of the use of deadly force. In addition to the recommendations made by the Secretary of State's Panel on Personal Protective Services in Iraq, beneficial changes include the initiative to move more military forces into the Iraqi provinces, and the subsequent policy changes initiated by Congress and implemented by the Departments of Defense and State. Another key improvement was the increased capability to conduct investigations (Commission on Wartime Contracting in Iraq and Afghanistan, 2009, p. 66).

Given these assessments, it appears that reforms aimed at improving the behavior of armed contractors with regard to Iraqi civilians have had at least a somewhat beneficial impact.

CHAPTER FIVE

Is There a Relative Lack of Unit Cohesion and Systematic Coordination Between Private Security Contractors and the Military?

The ability (or lack thereof) of private security contractors to coordinate successfully with U.S. military and coalition forces has been another topic of debate. A 2005 GAO report noted several problems in this area, despite efforts to improve:

> The relationship between the military and private security providers is one of coordination, not control. Prior to October 2004 coordination was informal, based on personal contacts, and was inconsistent. In October 2004 a Reconstruction Operations Center was opened to share intelligence and coordinate military-contractor interactions. While military and security providers agreed that coordination has improved, two problems remain. First, private security providers continue to report incidents between themselves and the military when approaching military convoys and checkpoints. Second, military units deploying to Iraq are not fully aware of the parties operating on the complex battle space in Iraq and what responsibility they have to those parties (GAO, 2005, Highlights).

Following up on the 2005 findings, a second GAO report noted in 2006:

> Coordination between the U.S. military and private security providers still needs improvement. First, private security providers continue to enter the battle space without coordinating with the U.S. military, putting both the military and security providers at a greater risk for injury. Second, U.S. military units are not trained, prior to deployment, on the operating procedures of private security providers in Iraq and the role of the Reconstruction Operations Center, which is to coordinate military-provider interactions. While DOD agreed with our prior recommendation to establish a pre-deployment training program to help address the coordination issue, no action has been taken (Government Accountability Office, 2006, Highlights).

At their extreme, problems of coordination between private security contractors and military troops in Iraq have resulted in friendly-fire, or so-called "blue-on-white," incidents. In a highly publicized case from May 2005, 16 contractors—all of them U.S. citizens, and many of them former Marines—working for Zapata Engineering were taken into Marine custody for three days for supposedly firing on a Marine watchtower at a military checkpoint (Phinney, 2005; Westervelt, 2005). While the contractors denied any wrongdoing, all were eventually fired and sent home because of the incident.

But statistics compiled by the Reconstruction Operations Center in Iraq indicate that the vast majority of reported blue-on-white incidents in Iraq are actually perpetrated by coalition forces against private security contractors, with most occurring when contractors are approaching checkpoints or passing military convoys.[1] A U.S. Army colonel working in the Department of Defense recounted one such incident:

> There was an incident about nine months ago, when a PMC team was going through Fallujah or somewhere. There were checkpoints all over. A reconstruction team with two civilians and one military guy went to check on the status of reconstruction. They went through the checkpoint three times. After going through twice without incident, the third time they got shot at by the checkpoint. There had been a guard change during which new guards were told to shoot at anything that wasn't a humvee. There are discrepancies between standards in the military. Sometimes they are only told to permit military convoys (confidential interview, 2006).

Such incidents strongly suggest a weakness in communications between contractors and the military in Iraq. Less extreme results of coordination problems have also been reported to be hindering the military's ability to accomplish its mission. For instance, occasions on which private security contractors failed to coordinate their movements with the relevant military commanders have, at times, reportedly led them to travel through unsecured areas where they have had to call on a military quick reaction force (QRF) for assistance when they encountered insurgents. Such incidents have drawn military units away from their other operations unexpectedly (Clark, 2008, citing the findings from 24 individual and small-group interviews conducted by the GAO between July 2004 and March 2006 for its 2005 and 2006 reports on "Actions Needed to Improve the Use of Private Security Providers").

Up to this point, the frequency with which such instances of failed coordination between teams of private security contractors and military units in Iraq actually occur has been unclear. Does the absence of systematic procedures to coordinate practices between the two groups mean that coordination is altogether absent? As noted in previous chapters, we have imposed a high threshold of expectations for armed

---

[1]   See the charts produced by the ROC Watch Officer reproduced in Clark, 2008, pp. 144–146.

contractors' behavior throughout this study because armed contractors' entire raison d'etre is to augment the force. Therefore, we view any evidence of a failure of PSCs to coordinate with the military as a cause for concern.

Sizable Minorities of Military and Diplomatic Personnel Indicate That Coordination Problems Between Contractors and the Military Are Not Absent

In light of the numerous reports of failed coordination between armed contractors and the military, the fact that most of the military personnel surveyed had fairly positive views on this issue is surprising. The majority had not seen firsthand any failures by private security contractors to coordinate with military commanders—70 percent of those who had no experience with contractors and 45 percent of those who did (Figure 5.1). However, those among the experienced group who had sometimes or rarely had firsthand knowledge of such failures were evenly split at 20 percent each, which is not a negligible figure considering our high expectations regarding contractor behavior.

A similar majority also had never seen armed contractors getting in the way of active-duty military personnel trying to perform their jobs (Figure 5.2). Again, however, the fact that 16 percent of those with experience interacting with contractors reported having sometimes observed such hindrances of military personnel, and 6 percent of this pool of respondents often had observed such hindrances, points to the need for improvement in interaction and coordination between PSCs and the military. Such data support the aforementioned reports focusing on PSC-military frictions.

Figure 5.1
Department of Defense Survey: Failure to Coordinate

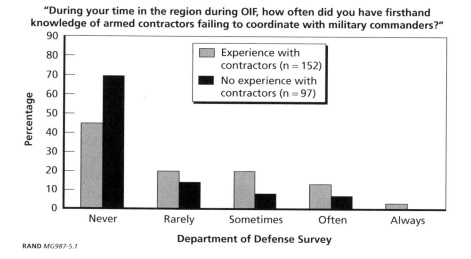

RAND MG987-5.1

Figure 5.2
Department of Defense Survey: Contractors Hindering Operations of Military

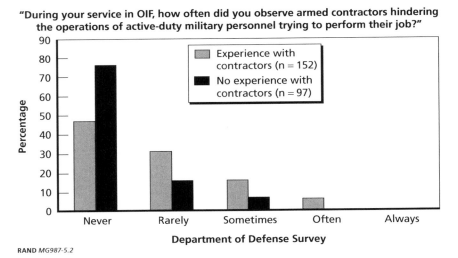

RAND *MG987-5.2*

Most military personnel felt that U.S. troops were generally doing their part to promote coordination. More than 80 percent of those inexperienced with contractors and half of those who had interacted with them had never observed military personnel impeding the operations of private security contractors (Figure 5.3). Such a high figure is not surprising, given the disincentives for military respondents to report fellow soldiers' shortcomings. What is surprising is that, in light of such disincentives, slightly more than 13 percent of those respondents with experience interacting with contractors

Figure 5.3
Department of Defense Survey: Military Hindering Operations of Contractors

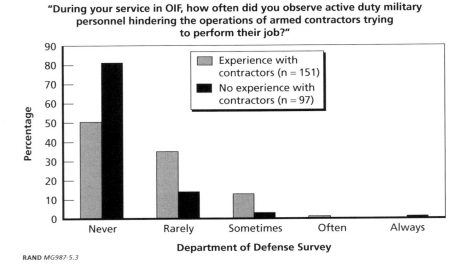

RAND *MG987-5.3*

reported having sometimes observed military personnel hindering PSC operations. This considerable figure speaks to the fact that coordination problems between armed contractors and the military stem not only from contractor failures to coordinate, but military failures to do so as well.

Therefore, although prevailing opinions within the military support the position that coordination between armed contractors and military units in Iraq is not lacking, the coordination that does occur may, indeed, not be systematic. Such a conclusion is in line with the findings of the 2005 GAO report: "[C]oordination was informal, based on personal contacts, and . . . inconsistent" (GAO, 2005). If coordination mainly occurs on an ad hoc basis, both contractors and the military can make an effort to work smoothly together even though they are not doing so in an organized or methodical manner. In this light, the question seems to be how great a need there is for a systematized approach to coordination—perhaps a direct communications channel—between commanders and armed contractors in theater.

State Department views reinforced those of the military, generally supporting the notion that the efforts of armed contractors and military personnel to work together smoothly went both ways. Nearly 60 percent of diplomatic personnel who had interacted with private security contractors believed that the contractors tried to coordinate well with the military; however, less than 25 percent of those who had not interacted held this view (Figure 5.4). Again, however, 16 percent of both the experienced and inexperienced groups of State Department respondents believed that it was typically false that armed contractors make an effort to work smoothly with U.S. military personnel. This is quite a considerable figure, considering that the armed contractors are intended to augment military forces.

Figure 5.4
Department of State Survey: Contractors Work Smoothly with the Military

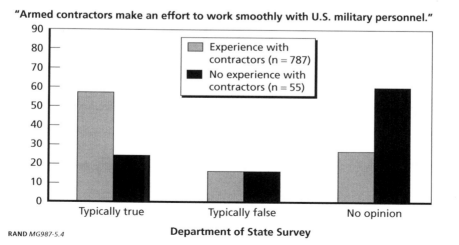

RAND *MG987-5.4*

Figure 5.5
Department of State Survey: The Military Works Smoothly with Contractors

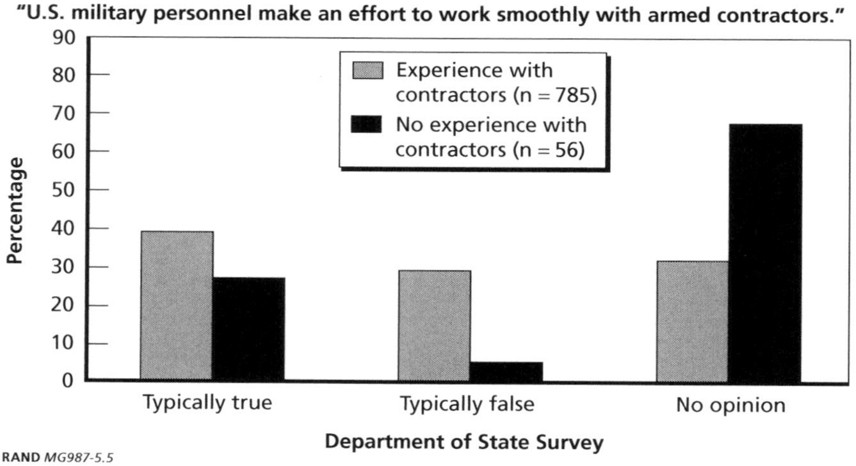

"U.S. military personnel make an effort to work smoothly with armed contractors."

RAND *MG987-5.5*

When it came to whether military personnel make a similar effort, the majority of State Department respondents felt that they did. But here the gap between those experienced respondents feeling such a statement was true and those thinking it to be false was much more narrow than in the military survey: Whereas almost 40 percent of DoS personnel thought U.S. military personnel make an effort to work smoothly with armed contractors, nearly 30 percent felt the opposite (Figure 5.5). Interestingly, however, this gap was much wider for those DoS personnel without experience interacting with armed contractors, with 27 percent feeling that military personnel make such an effort and only 5 percent feeling that they do not (and 68 percent having no opinion). This speaks to the possibility that respondents' background knowledge and opinions of the military as a professional force (and hence, one likely to make efforts to work with PSCs) shaped their survey responses when they had less direct experience interacting with armed contractors.

In terms of armed contractors' efforts to work well with the diplomatic community in Iraq, a greater number of State Department respondents thought that contractors work well with diplomatic personnel than thought they work smoothly with military personnel. Eighty percent of those who had sometimes or often interacted with armed contractors and nearly 40 percent of those who had never or rarely interacted with armed contractors thought this was true (Figure 5.6). This distinction is probably due to the fact that many private security contractors work directly on a daily basis with State Department personnel as their bodyguards. But the perception that they make a greater *effort* to work well with diplomatic personnel than they do with military personnel is nonetheless interesting.

All in all, it appears that a majority of both military and DoS personnel perceive that armed contractors and the military interact fairly competently. Yet, considerable

Figure 5.6
Department of State Survey: Contractors Work Smoothly with State

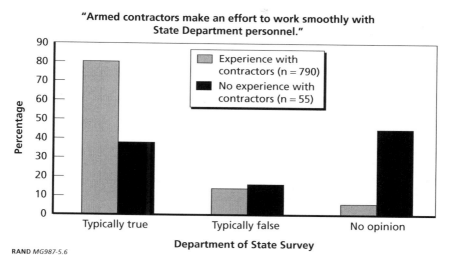

RAND *MG987-5.6*

minorities of each group note coordination problems on behalf of both PSCs and the military with regard to their interactions with each other. Such evidence supports numerous earlier reports detailing PSC-military coordination problems in Iraq and speaks to the fact that the lack of systematic coordination procedures is probably to blame for these coordination problems, rather than the failings of either group in particular.

CHAPTER SIX

Do Private Security Contractors Play a Valuable Supporting Role to the U.S. Military as a Force Multiplier?

As we have noted throughout this report, contractors have become an institutionalized addition to U.S. military forces over the past few decades due to their supposedly beneficial effects on the force. Indeed, Army Field Manual (FM) 3-100.21 considers contractors to provide a valuable means of augmenting capabilities and to generate a force multiplier effect (Department of the Army, 1999). Greater support from contractors permits the Army to deploy fewer combat service support personnel and allows the operational commander greater leeway in designing a force. Experiences from the Balkans provide a vivid example: Increasing levels of contractor support and smaller numbers of military logistical support personnel were able to successfully produce more "tooth" and less "tail" (Palmer, 1999). When both logistical support contractors and private security contractors substituted for military support units, more combat units could be deployed:

> In Bosnia . . . the Army replaced soldiers at the gate and base perimeter with contracted security guards. In Kosovo, the Army replaced its firefighters with contracted firefighters as the number of troops authorized to be in Kosovo decreased. By using contractors, the military maximizes its combat forces in an area (GAO, 2003, p. 8).

Before Iraq, most force multiplier experiences entailed replacing combat troops with unarmed contractors in a generally stable environment. According to one view, private security contractors produce the very same effect when they perform security tasks in the unstable setting of Operation Iraqi Freedom. Leon Sharon, a representative of Falcon Security, explains:

> All of the work that's being conducted here in Iraq by private security companies would have to be conducted by somebody, and that somebody is U.S. military personnel. . . . If you had 500 soldiers here, that's 500 less soldiers that you have on the battlefield (Fainaru, 2007b, p. A01).

In a similar vein, General David Petraeus emphasized private security contractors' contribution to the U.S. mission in Iraq when testifying before Congress:

> [T]ens of thousands of contract security forces and ministerial security forces… do in fact guard facilities and secure institutions and so forth that our forces, coalition or Iraqi forces, would otherwise have to guard and secure (Committee on Armed Services, 2007, p. 17).

This school of thought holds that when private security contractors provide bodyguards and nonmilitary site and convoy security, they relieve soldiers from having to perform these duties. In this way, employing private security contractors generates advantages similar to using unarmed contractors as substitutes for regular troops (Garcia-Perez, 1999; Schreier and Caparini, 2005).

But skeptics hold that the operations of private security contractors may inadvertently place additional strain on the armed forces, because at times when armed contractors engage the enemy in the course of their work, they may require rapid support from the military.[1] On one occasion, for example, private security contractors reportedly escorted a local CPA administrator into Najaf during a military operation without the knowledge of the local commander. When the administrator and the security team got involved in a firefight, the military had to send in troops. This incident had a significant impact on the operation that had been in progress (GAO, 2005).

The procedures associated with military assistance to private security contractors were even formalized within the Reconstruction Operations Centers (ROCs), the coordination hubs for contractors and coalition forces that were established across Iraq in 2004. The policy dictates that, should contractors be in need of assistance such as a quick reaction force or medical help, the military is to provide it (assuming resources are available). Just such an event occurred in February 2005, when insurgents ambushed a private security team. The contractors contacted the ROC, the military sent in a QRF and the team was escorted safely back to Mosul. In another case, U.S. forces responded to a call from private security contractors, using helicopters to provide air cover and AC-130 gunships for close air support (Pelton, 2007).

In short, according to this school of thought, private security contractors can at times cause more strain than relief for the armed forces, because they may need to be bailed out when under attack. However, because we have set a high threshold of expectations for armed contractors' behavior and contributions to U.S. and coalition forces, we view any evidence to support this more pessimistic view of contractors' contributions as troubling.

---

[1] This strain is in addition to the demands already placed on the armed forces to protect unarmed civilian contractors. A vast amount of military force is needed to provide protection for all civilians working in the theater of operations—at least those under DoD contract (Nelson, 2000; Orsini and Bublitz, 1999; Urey, 2005).

Both Military and Diplomatic Personnel Tend to View Armed Contractors as Force Multipliers, but a Considerable Minority of Respondents Feels Differently

Personnel within both the military and the State Department tended to consider private security contractors as a force multiplier rather than an additional strain on military troops, although such a feeling was much more pronounced among those respondents who had direct experience with armed contractors. Nonetheless, even when considering only those respondents without experience interacting with contractors, a much larger number of both military and DoS respondents felt that it was true that armed contractors constituted force multipliers than those who felt that such a statement was false. Within both the military and diplomatic groups of respondents, those without direct experience interacting with contractors were more likely to answer that they had "no opinion" on this issue than they were to say that it was "typically false" that armed contractors were force multipliers for the U.S. military.

Within the Department of Defense, two-thirds of surveyed personnel with experience of armed contractors, but only 40 percent of those who lacked that experience, felt it was typically true that contractors were a means of enabling more combat units to be deployed (Figure 6.1). Many fewer felt that it was typically false that armed contractors are force multipliers, with only 21 percent and 27 percent of both the experienced and inexperienced groups, respectively, holding this view. Nonetheless, as noted above, because the Department of Defense integrated contractors into the U.S. force structure due to their effects in augmenting the force, we set a high threshold of expectations for contractors' contributions to the force (Department of Defense 1990). Therefore, it is somewhat surprising that 21 percent and 27 percent of those military

Figure 6.1
Department of Defense Survey: Armed Contractors as Force Multipliers

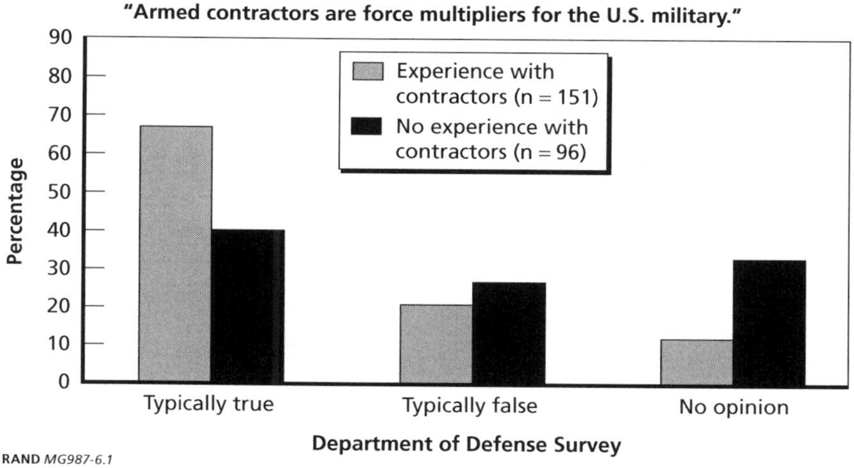

RAND MG987-6.1

Figure 6.2
Department of State Survey: Armed Contractors as Force Multipliers

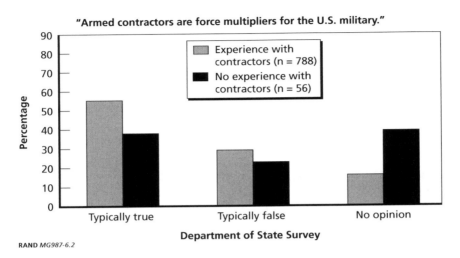

"Armed contractors are force multipliers for the U.S. military."

Legend:
- Experience with contractors (n = 788)
- No experience with contractors (n = 56)

Department of State Survey

RAND *MG987-6.2*

respondents with and without direct experience interacting with armed contractors, respectively, feel that armed contractors do *not* constitute force multipliers.

More than 50 percent of State Department personnel with experience interacting with armed contractors similarly answered that it was typically true that armed contractors were force multipliers, but slightly less than 40 percent without contractor experience felt this way (Figure 6.2). As with the military, between 20 percent and 30 percent of both those diplomatic respondents with and without experience interacting with armed contractors (29 percent and 23 percent, respectively) felt that armed contractors were not force multipliers. Again, given the fact that one of the most basic rationales for using armed contractors is their force multiplying effect, the presence of this rather large minority feeling that such an effect is absent is disconcerting. Of those groups of personnel experienced with contractors in both the military and the State Department, those in the military tended to feel more strongly that armed contractors constituted force multipliers than did their diplomatic counterparts.

However, relatively few military personnel reported having had to provide a QRF to come to the aid of armed contractors (Figure 6.3), with nearly 60 percent of those with experience interacting with contractors never having had to provide a QRF for contractors. This is to be expected, however; because contractors are deployed to augment the force, we would not expect to have to devote military resources to bail them out of trouble very often. The fact that more than 10 percent of military respondents with direct contractor experience reported sometimes having had to provide such aid to armed contractors speaks to a potential inefficiency in side-by-side contractor-military deployments, because it indicates that armed contractors can, at times, distract the military from its other aims.

Figure 6.3
Department of Defense Survey: Frequency of Needing to Provide QRFs to Aid Armed Contractors

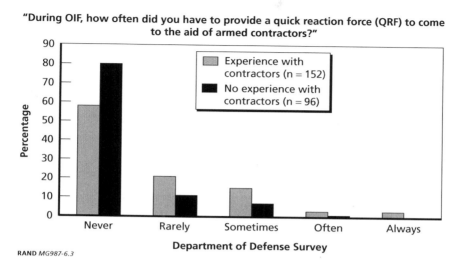

"During OIF, how often did you have to provide a quick reaction force (QRF) to come to the aid of armed contractors?"

Legend:
- Experience with contractors (n = 152)
- No experience with contractors (n = 96)

Department of Defense Survey

In short, private security contractors are generally viewed as a welcome force multiplier by many military and diplomatic personnel, and troops who had had more contact with them were the most positive about their contributions in this area. Given our expectations that armed contractors will augment the force, this is not surprising. At the same time, however, it is troubling that considerable minorities of both military and diplomatic personnel viewed armed contractors as *not* constituting a force multiplier, and a sizable number of military respondents reported having had to come to the aid of PSCs on occasion. Such data indicate that anecdotal reports skeptical of the value of armed contractors are not completely unfounded.

CHAPTER SEVEN

Do Private Security Contractors Provide Skills and Services That the Armed Forces Lack?

From one standpoint, the employment of private security contractors can provide the United States with access to capabilities that would otherwise be unavailable or "would [either] take an inordinate amount of time to develop internally, or . . . be prohibitively expensive to develop" (Wynn, 2004, p. 4). Proponents of this "valuable skills" argument claim that although the vast majority of private security contractors provide services that the military itself is designed to perform, a small segment of this group of contractors might be able to offer additional skills.[1] Aside from basic guard services, private security contractors also provide highly specialized personal security details and bring a background to the job that most soldiers do not have. David Isenberg points out that many of these armed civilians are not merely ex-military, but former members of elite units—Rangers, Green Berets, Delta Force, SEALs, Special Air Service, or Special Boat Service:

> In the role of security operator, they are able to bring a lifetime of training and experience to a specific job. Most of the actual security teams operating on the ground frequently are composed of former and retired senior NCOs, men in their 30s and early 40s. This level of experience contributes to a more relaxed environment that simplifies operations. Leaders trust their operators to ensure basic tasks have been performed as second nature, and that their staff is highly professional and disciplined. In contrast a young Army soldier or Marine, recently graduated from his or her basic training and specialty school is just that: young and inexperienced (Isenberg, 2009, pp. 43–44).

However, a common objection to the valuable skills argument is that it is far from certain that contractors will actually deliver these high-quality services. Behind this skepticism lies the assumption that, because private security contractors are profit-driven entities, they may not comply with their contracts if they see a better

---

[1] The "valuable skills" argument seems to hold true in other areas of contracting—for example, high-tech weapon systems. The armed forces often lack the knowledge base to maintain or even operate these systems. For instance, contractors maintained the Apache and Blackhawk helicopters in Bosnia due to a lack of organic maintenance capabilities (GAO, 2003). A handful of developmental/operational test pilots and contractor pilots were the only personnel available to operate Global Hawk Unmanned Aerial Vehicles in Iraq (Guidry and Wills, 2004).

chance of maximizing profits (Stoeber, 2007). About one firm, for example, the Special Inspector General for Iraq Reconstruction reported, "there is no assurance that Aegis is providing the best possible safety and security for government and reconstruction personnel and facilities" (Special Inspector General for Iraq Reconstruction, 2005, p. i).[2] That said, neither Blackwater/Xe, which provided security for the U.S. Departments of Defense and State, nor Aegis and Erinys, which guard the Army Corps of Engineers, have lost a client to enemy fire yet (Committee on Oversight and Government Reform, 2007a; Fainaru, 2007c). Because we have set a high threshold of expectations for armed contractors' behavior and contributions to the force in this monograph, we expect that military and DoS respondents will view armed contractors as providing valuable skills. Indeed, any considerable evidence to the contrary is cause for concern, for it indicates that one of the rationales for utilizing armed contractors may be mistaken.

Military and Diplomatic Personnel Tend to View Armed Contractors as Providing Valuable Skills

Within the military, on the whole, personnel tend to think that armed contractors do provide valuable skill sets to the U.S. government (Figure 7.1). When survey respondents who felt that armed contractors sometimes, often, or always add valuable skills are considered together, a majority deemed the contribution of contractors in this area to be positive. Both those with and without experience with armed contractors held similar views on this issue, with 92 percent and 93 percent respectively giving an answer in one of these three categories. Only a negligible few felt that armed contractors never provided valuable skills.

Figure 7.1
Department of Defense Survey: Valuable Skill Sets

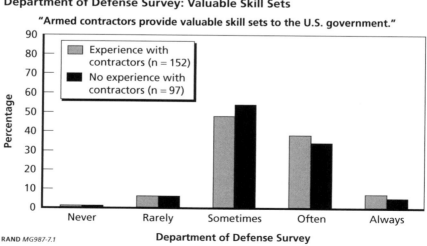

RAND MG987-7.1

---

[2]   Aegis is a private security firm based in the United Kingdom.

Figure 7.2
Department of State Survey: Valuable Skill Sets

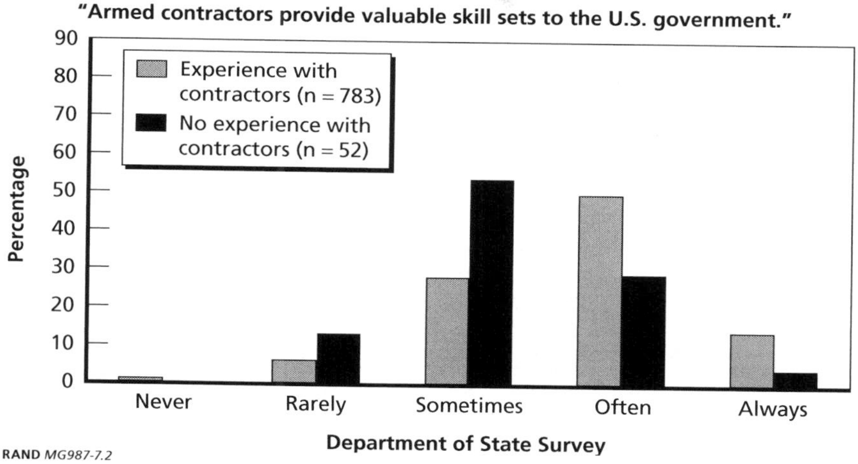

"Armed contractors provide valuable skill sets to the U.S. government."

RAND MG987-7.2

In the State Department, the overall view on this issue was also highly positive (Figure 7.2). Ninety-two percent of those experienced with contractors and 87 percent of those with little or no experience felt that these armed personnel sometimes, often, or always provide the government with valuable skill sets. Nearly half of those respondents experienced with contractors considered the contribution to occur often. This suggests that diplomatic personnel, particularly those with direct experience interacting with armed contractors, placed even more value on the skills added by armed contractors than did their military counterparts (whose most common answer, in contrast, was "sometimes"). But taking the two groups of State Department personnel separately, it was those experienced with contractors who were more likely to answer "often" or "always." Personnel without contact with contractors were more likely to see them as only sometimes contributing valuable skills. Again, as with the military sample, only a negligible few DoS respondents felt that armed contractors never provided valuable skills to the U.S. government.

Evaluating whether private security contractors contribute to U.S. foreign policy objectives is even more important. Among military and State Department personnel alike, the clear majority consider armed contractors to make both negative and positive contributions: In total, 62 percent of the surveyed military personnel and 67 percent of the State Department respondents held this view. In the military, though, most of the remainder (23 percent) considered them to be contributing positively, while on the diplomatic side, opinions among the remainder as to whether the contributions were negative or positive were nearly split (16 percent versus 14 percent). Considering that we expect armed contractors to augment the force, such numbers indicating that DoS personnel view them as negatively contributing to U.S. foreign policy objectives are rather troubling.

Figure 7.3
Department of Defense Survey: Contributions to Foreign Policy

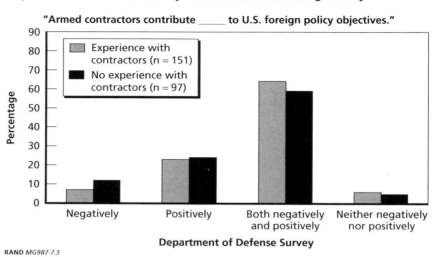

These trends remain consistent when we look at the opinions of those military respondents experienced with contractors and those not (Figure 7.3). The unquestioned majority—nearly two-thirds—of both groups judged the contributions to foreign policy objectives to be mixed. About one-quarter held them to be positive.

Diplomatic personnel also did not break with the overall trends when viewed as two separate groups (Figure 7.4). The vast majority—68 percent of those experienced with contractors and 63 percent of the inexperienced—considered the contributions of private security contractors to foreign policy objectives to be both positive and negative. Outside this majority, slightly more than 10 percent had positive views on the

Figure 7.4
Department of State Survey: Foreign Policy

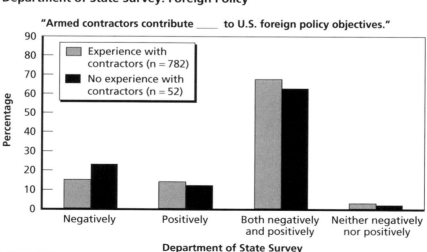

contributions to U.S. foreign policy, while a slightly larger percentage of both experienced and inexperienced diplomatic respondents held a negative view of armed contractors on this issue.

In sum, the skill sets and services that private security contractors provide to the armed forces are highly valued by both military and State Department personnel, with the diplomatic group holding those skills in even higher regard than the military does. This trend becomes even stronger when comparing only personnel who have had experience with armed contractors across the Departments of Defense and State. But viewed in terms of the contribution that armed contractors are making to U.S. foreign policy objectives, opinions are much more mixed, with a clear majority of both military and diplomatic personnel regarding those contributions as both positive and negative, and a nonnegligible minority of State Department respondents viewing them as primarily negative. Given that we have a high threshold of expectations for armed contractors' behavior and contributions to the force, such data provide cause for concern. However, in light of the evidence of military and DoS perceptions regarding armed contractors' impact on Iraqi civilians highlighted in Chapter Four, these data regarding their perceptions of PSCs' impacts on U.S. foreign policy objectives are not overly surprising. As with the question of whether armed contractors are force multipliers, the data indicate that anecdotal reports skeptical of the value of armed contractors are not completely unfounded.

Do Private Security Contractors Provide Vital Surge Capacity and Critical Security Services?

For those who take a favorable view of private military contractors, one important contribution is their perceived ability to provide surge capacity to the U.S. armed forces (Avant, 2005; Fredland, 2004; Zamparelli, 1999). Although this argument usually refers to contractors who provide logistical support, it has recently also been extended to private security contractors. Marion Bowman, for instance, observes:

> Iraq provides an example of how that surge capability functions in the contemporary battlespace. As the conflict loomed in 2003, it was clear that combat in Iraq would entail private security industry capabilities (Bowman, 2007).

Two examples illustrate the extent to which private security contractors are able to play this role. By July 2004, just two firms alone—Aegis Defence Services and Erinys Iraq—had placed about 2,000 employees in Iraq, a force the size of three military battalions (Fainaru, 2007c). When the U.S. Army brought in additional troops in 2007, private security companies conducted a parallel surge, boosting manpower and adding expensive armor (Fainaru, 2007b).

Opinions that support this viewpoint can be found both inside and out of government. The GAO has formally stated that private security contractors are necessary to the Iraq mission, reporting that they fulfill important security functions throughout the country in support of the Department of Defense's military mission and the State Department's diplomatic mission (GAO, 2008). A high-ranking official in the Department of Defense has informally sanctioned this view, stating, "We need [private security] contractors. They are enablers" (confidential interview, 2006). State Department personnel have also endorsed it. For example, Department of State Deputy Assistant Secretary Greg Starr testified to Congress:

> [O]ur ability to provide protective operations on the scale required in this environment would not have been possible without using private security contractors. The number of personnel security specialists we utilize in Iraq alone is more than all the

diplomatic security agents we have globally. We could not have trained and hired new agents to meet this requirement as rapidly as the contractors met the requirement... (Committee on Government Reform, 2006, p. 45).[1]

From the contractor side, similar opinions are common. Graham Kerr, chief operating officer of Hart Security, for instance, considers the contributions of private security contractors as absolutely necessary to operations in Iraq. In his view, the U.S. armed forces cannot carry out operations there autonomously (Kerr, 2008).

Nonetheless, skeptics counter that what armed contractors can add to surge capacity is of little value, since their reliability is doubtful:

> The closer contractors are to the battlefield, the more they run the risk of getting in "harm's way." A calculation . . . comparing what the costs of getting into harm are with the costs of withdrawing, may actually make it more attractive not to provide a service (Leander, 2006, p. 79).

This opinion may originate from experience with unarmed contractors providing logistics services. In the first Persian Gulf War, for example, support from this subset of contractors was far from perfect. Contracted drivers were not reliable; indeed, they would fall behind schedule, forcing soldiers to replace them to avoid the danger of mass defection (Schreier and Caparini, 2005). Some contractors providing food service at several Air Force installations simply walked away from their jobs after hearing of chemical-attack warnings (Dowling and Feck, 1999). Many civilian contractors refused to be deployed to the country's most dangerous areas, leaving soldiers lacking fresh food, showers, and toilets for months (Bianco and Forest, 2003).

Armed contractors who directly engage with the enemy are, indeed, often in harm's way and could present costs high enough to warrant careful thought about whether to use them. But that said, there are no accounts of armed contractors showing a lack of reliability in terms of reluctance to enter insecure areas or to do their jobs when under threat. On the contrary, private security contractors held the ground when the facilities of the Coalition Provisional Authority came under attack in Al Kut in April 2003 and in Najaf in April 2004 (Priest, 2004; Pelton, 2007). The central question, in short, is whether the surge capacity and security services that armed contractors have provided in Iraq have been an important part of the operation. As in earlier chapters, because we impose a high threshold of expectations for armed contractors' abilities to augment the force, we generally expect that military and State Department personnel will view armed contractors as providing surge capacity for the U.S.

---

[1]   Another advocate of this point of view, Peter Singer, has gone so far as to claim that the Iraq operation would not be possible without the support of private security contractors. But he attributes this not so much to the ability of armed contractors to supplement military resources, as to the idea that the deployment of private security contractors draws much less public attention than that of troops, which, he argues, helps make the Iraq operation more politically feasible (Singer, 2007, p. 4).

government. Yet, because armed contractors may augment the force without necessarily providing it with the capacity to "surge," our threshold of expectations is not quite as high here as in earlier chapters of this monograph. Furthermore, because the survey questions were worded to ask whether or not armed contractors provided "necessary" surge capacity for the U.S. government, we do not view negative responses from either groups of respondents with as much concern as we did in previous chapters. Indeed, if they felt such surge capacity was unnecessary, respondents may have answered negatively even if they perceived PSCs to be providing that capacity.

Military and Diplomatic Personnel Tend to View Armed Contractors as Providing Necessary Surge Capacity and Critical Security Services

In general, military and State Department personnel believe strongly that armed contractors do provide needed surge capacity. Within the military, 62 percent of those with experience with armed contractors held this view, whereas that sense was even stronger among the diplomatic community, with 75 percent of experienced respondents feeling this way (Figures 8.1 and 8.2). Those in the Department of Defense with no experience interacting with armed contractors were only about half as likely to agree, with 34 percent feeling this way. While 18 percent of military respondents with experience with armed contractors felt that they did not provide needed surge capacity for the U.S. government, we are not overly concerned about this negative response due to the possibility that some of these respondents simply did not view such surge capacity as a necessity.

The State Department sample also showed a sizable split between experienced and inexperienced respondents. Three-quarters of those with experience interacting

Figure 8.1
Department of Defense Survey: Surge Capacity

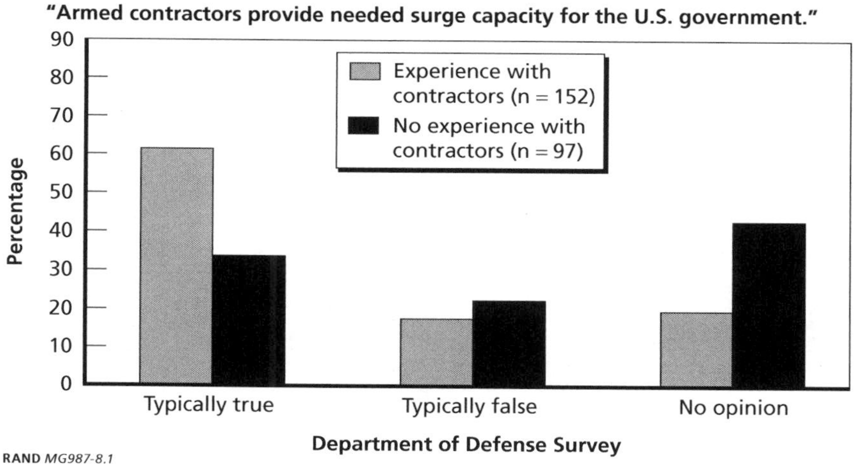

"Armed contractors provide needed surge capacity for the U.S. government."

Figure 8.2
Department of State Survey: Surge Capacity

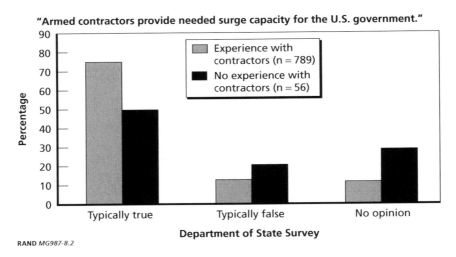

RAND *MG987-8.2*

with armed contractors and half of those without such experience considered armed contractors to provide vital surge capacity (Figure 8.2).[2]

The value that armed contractors are perceived to add in this area goes beyond surge capacity for combat operations. The majority of both those military and diplomatic personnel with experience with armed contractors also think that they provide security critical to the success of reconstruction projects (Figures 8.3 and 8.4). Indeed, 69 percent of those military respondents with experience interacting with armed contractors felt this to be true, while only 17 percent felt it to be false.

The gap in responses among the State Department respondents with experience interacting with armed contractors was even wider, with 77 percent of this group considering PSCs to make a critical contribution to reconstruction and only about 12 percent feeling that they do not make such a contribution. Although the percentage was lower among those without direct experience with armed contractors, slightly more than 50 percent of this group still felt that armed contractors provided security critical to the success of reconstruction projects (Figure 8.4).

In sum, private security contractors are welcomed by both the State Department and the military as providing surge capacity and critical security. Personnel who have interacted with armed contractors more frequently tend to perceive their contributions in these areas to be more positive than those who have not.[3] Furthermore, experienced

---

[2]   On the whole, contractor-inexperienced State Department and military personnel were less prone than experienced personnel to assess PSCs as a surge capacity (military: 17 percent; State Department: 15 percent).

[3]   There seems to be a general trend that the group having experience with armed contractors perceived PSCs more positively, although at times this experience afforded respondents the opportunity to witness PSCs' abuses of their position and subsequently resulted in negative perceptions. The numbers seem to indicate that proximity

Figure 8.3
Department of Defense Survey: Reconstruction

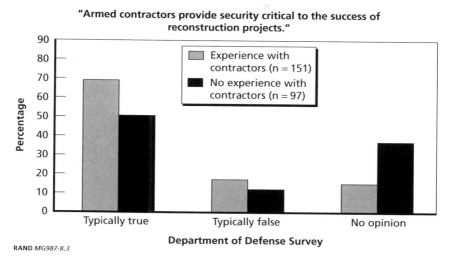

RAND *MG987-8.3*

Figure 8.4
Department of State Survey: Reconstruction

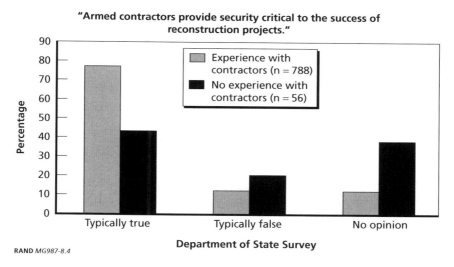

RAND *MG987-8.4*

State Department personnel consider armed contractors favorably on these issues more often than do their military counterparts.

to contractors and the experience of interacting with them has a strong influence on the perception. The results need to be treated very carefully, however, since the total number of respondents with and without contractor experience is not equal and the total number of inexperienced respondents is often very small.

CHAPTER NINE

Summary of Findings and Policy Recommendations

When it comes to issues of pay disparity, legal accountability, and PSC-military coordination, it is clear that military and State Department personnel perceive PSCs both to have imposed costs on U.S. military operations in Iraq and to have provided benefits to these operations. Both military and State Department personnel believe that the pay disparity between contractors and the military has a negative impact on military recruitment, retention, and morale, although actual military continuation rates do not reflect such a negative impact. If it does exist to any extent, military reenlistment bonuses may reduce it somewhat. Most State Department respondents thought that armed contractors were not typically respectful of local and international laws and that armed contractors do not display an understanding and sensitivity to the Iraqi people and their culture. Furthermore—despite the fact that only 12 percent of DoS respondents who had deployed once to Iraq and 18 percent of those deployed twice or more reported sometimes having firsthand knowledge of armed contractors mistreating Iraqi civilians—this number is fairly troubling because of our high threshold of expectations regarding armed contractors' behavior toward civilians. However, the majority of DoS respondents do not believe that armed contractors are given free reign to misbehave with little accountability.

With regard to PSC-military coordination, a majority of military respondents reported never having had any firsthand knowledge of armed contractors failing to coordinate with military commanders or having ever observed armed contractors hindering the operations of active-duty military personnel trying to perform their job. On both issues, however, increased exposure to PSCs made it more likely that the respondent had such knowledge or had observed such behavior. Furthermore, a majority of military respondents reported never having observed military personnel hindering the operations of armed contractors trying to perform their job. All these findings bode well for PSC-military coordination. Meanwhile, a majority of DoS respondents thought that armed contractors make an effort to work smoothly with U.S. military personnel. A particularly interesting finding with regard to coordination issues is the fact that a much higher percentage of DoS respondents thought that armed contractors make an effort to work smoothly with DoS personnel than those who thought that armed contractors make an effort to work smoothly with military personnel.

Finally, it is worth emphasizing that the survey data show that increased exposure to PSCs has both a positive and negative impact on one's views of PSCs. Greater levels of interaction with PSCs afforded respondents the opportunity both to witness PSCs' abuses of their position and other negative traits and to gain an appreciation for the positive work that PSCs do. Progress can continue to be made to improve perceptions of PSC deployment situations if policies are instituted to correct PSCs' negative traits and if others' exposure to them continues to increase over time.

The differences between the perceptions of the State Department and military personnel seem to follow another pattern wherein the perception of the different roles of PSCs is influenced by the respective needs of the military and the State Department. The more a particular group uses armed contractors in a particular role, the more positively the group perceives them. For instance, the military uses PSCs mostly as force multipliers. In other areas, their contributions are not necessarily needed. For instance, PSC skills might only be of limited value and their contribution to security might be less crucial to the armed forces.

This is different for the State Department respondents, who found that PSCs were critical for the protection of their personnel and for the provision of organic capabilities not otherwise available in sufficient numbers. Thus, State Department and military personnel tended to welcome the contributions by PSCs more in the areas where they each had special needs that could be met by contractors. However, despite the differences in each group's perception of PSCs, both seem to agree that armed contractors in Iraq have neither a solely negative nor a solely beneficial impact on U.S. operations in the theater. Indeed, while majorities of both groups of respondents often viewed PSCs in a relatively positive—or at least benign—light, sizable minorities often reported negative perceptions of armed contractors on a variety of issues. Such minority views should not be overlooked; indeed, they are troubling given our high threshold of expectations for armed contractor contributions to U.S. forces (which, in turn, is based on the U.S. government's rationale for integrating contractors into the force). Whether the costs of PSC use outweigh the benefits is a question open to subjective interpretation that this study does not attempt to answer. However, it is clear that—given the prolific use of armed contractors alongside the U.S. military in modern contingencies—measures aimed at ameliorating the negative impacts of armed contractors would benefit future U.S. military operations.

Recommendations

Based on these findings, several recommendations are in order. First, steps must be taken to alleviate the negative impact of contractor pay on military morale. An improved military predeployment training regimen regarding contractor functions, including recommendations for how to interact with contractors, could help to increase the level of understanding and cohesion between contractors and the military in the field and thus counteract the impact of contractor pay on military morale.

Second, despite the fact that most military and DoS respondents do not believe that PSCs are free to misbehave with little accountability, DoS personnel clearly believe that contractors do not respect local and international laws and that they do not display an understanding and sensitivity to the Iraqi people and their culture. Further legal regulation could therefore be useful. The SOFA's extension of Iraqi legal jurisdiction to U.S. and third-country national contractors operating in Iraq might help to alleviate problems associated with contractor recklessness and the associated impact of contractor operations on Iraqi civilians. However, because of the fairly undeveloped Iraqi legal system, a working U.S. domestic legal system of prosecuting contractor abuses is preferable to the prosecution of contractors under Iraqi law. A continued willingness by the Department of Justice to effectively use the revised MEJA to prosecute contractor abuses is therefore advisable. Given the large number of armed contractors likely to deploy in support of future U.S. military operations, however, policymakers should recognize that taking this recommendation seriously will likely entail larger demands for military police and officers in the Judge Advocate General Corps to be able to enforce U.S. laws as they apply to contractors. Another option is the conscientious use of contract law, which already covers contractors, to bring their behavior under a different control regime. This might prove to be a relatively simple fix, requiring only that contracting officers systematize the behavioral requirements for PSCs as written into their contracts.

The Reconstruction Operations Center is an institutional mechanism that can and should be replicated in other theaters where contractors and the military are required to work together in large numbers, to streamline communications between the two groups. The blue-force tracker system is another mechanism that has been successful in standardizing communications between the two groups, and participation in the system should be mandated for all contractors operating in a country where U.S. forces are operating. While ad hoc coordination appears to occur on a fairly regular basis, standardizing PSC-military coordination practices will better ensure that armed contractors have a primarily positive impact on the U.S. military mission.

Any weakness in communications between contractors and the military in Iraq could readily be improved by the distribution of military radios to all contracting teams operating in theater (Clark, 2008). The benefits of such improvements in PSC-military communication were seen during the introduction of the blue-force tracker system to contractor operations. This system had a very beneficial impact on PSC-military coordination for those contractors who chose to participate in it (confidential interview, 2006). An extension of the blue-force tracker program to contractors in other theaters is therefore worth considering.

Blue-on-white incidents also speak to the problem of the lack of a requirement that contractors wear standardized, identifiable uniforms. Although some private military and security firms do require that their personnel wear standardized uniforms with identifying insignia, others do not, making it difficult at times for the military to identify contractors as friendly forces. The presence of uniforms also impacts contractors' combatant status under international law, affecting, among other things, whether they can be considered POWs and whether they can legally participate in hostilities (Cameron, 2006). Furthermore, in an environment of insurgency, such as the Iraq war, enemy forces can disguise themselves as contractors (especially as local nationals working for contracting firms), complicating the issue of proper identification. The issue of contractors' uniforms therefore has both a practical and a legal implication.

Duties Best Filled by Contractors

Both the military and State Department surveys are instructive in terms of prescribing appropriate future roles for armed contractors. Both surveys asked respondents to rank up to six choices on a list of "duties best filled by contractors." Because the Commission on Wartime Contracting in Iraq and Afghanistan considers private security contractors to be those contractors providing personal security, convoy security, and static security services, we have chosen to emphasize these contractors and closely related security activities here (Commission on Wartime Contracting in Iraq and Afghanistan, 2009). Out of these activities, the most frequently selected duties from the military sample were: "protection of property" (selected by 41 percent of military respondents), "prison oversight" (selected by 37 percent of military respondents), "convoy escort" (selected by 36 percent of military respondents), and "protection of personnel" (also selected by 36 percent of military respondents). The lowest-ranked duties selected by military respondents included "combat" (selected by 4 percent of respondents), "fighting counterinsurgency" (selected by 6 percent of respondents), and "enforcement of law and order" (selected by 14 percent of respondents).

The responses of State Department respondents largely mirror those of the military, although the order in which the duties were ranked differs somewhat. DoS respondents indicated the following to be appropriate duties for armed contractors: "protection of property" (selected by 63 percent of DoS respondents), "protection of personnel" (selected by 56 percent of DoS respondents), and "convoy escort" (selected by 51 percent of DoS respondents). Interestingly, State Department respondents did not, on the whole, agree with military respondents that "prison oversight" was an appropriate duty for armed contractors, with only 19 percent of DoS respondents selecting it.

Differences between the responses of all DoS and military respondents and those military and DoS respondents with direct experience interacting with armed contractors are worth noting. Interestingly, both military and State Department respondents with direct experience chose the same top duties for armed contractors, although with slight differences in the order of those top duties between the two groups. Forty percent of experienced military respondents chose "protection of property," 39 percent chose "protection of personnel," and 36 percent chose "convoy escort." Note that the pool of military respondents with experience with armed contractors did not choose "prison oversight" as an appropriate duty for armed contractors, while the larger pool of military respondents did. The lowest-ranked duties for armed contractors, according to military respondents with experience interacting with them, were "combat" (selected by only 4 percent of military respondents), "fighting counterinsurgency" (selected by 7 percent), "enforcement of law and order" (selected by 12 percent), and "interrogation" (selected by 18 percent).

State Department respondents with experience interacting with armed contractors, on the other hand, ranked the following as duties best filled by armed contractors: "protection of property" (selected by 66 percent of DoS respondents), "protection of personnel" (selected by 58 percent), and "convoy escort" (selected by 53 percent). Experienced DoS respondents' answers mirrored those of military respondents in terms of the lowest-ranked duties for armed contractors, although in different proportions: only 0.5 percent selected "combat," 2 percent selected "fighting counterinsurgency," 4 percent selected "interrogation," and 7 percent selected "enforcement of law and order."

The results of the surveys therefore indicate that—in the opinions of the military and DoS personnel working alongside PSCs—certain duties are more appropriate to PSCs than are others, whatever future contingencies they may find themselves in. Those with the most direct experience with armed contractors viewed protection of property and personnel and convoy escort as the most appropriate future roles for private security contractors. Meanwhile, direct combat and associated functions (such as fighting counterinsurgency, enforcement of law and order, and interrogation) were perceived to be best relegated to state-run military and police forces.

Methodology

Despite the number of PSCs under contract in OIF, there is a dearth of primary data available to analysts and policymakers on the topic. Instead, most analyses depend on interviews, anecdotal reporting, and indirect insights into the relative benefits and challenges of using armed contractors. This project sought to fill a portion of that knowledge gap by fielding surveys to gain direct insights into the perspectives of those in the field who work directly with PSCs.

After conducting a few dozen interviews over several months with subject-matter experts, we were able to develop hypotheses about armed contractors that we could test with a survey of active-duty military personnel. Interviewees included a deputy undersecretary of defense, an assistant secretary of state, a chief executive officer of a prominent PSC, active and retired armed contractors, analysts, trade associations, and employees of DoD (Office of the Assistant Secretary of Defense for Special Operations and Low Intensity Conflict, the Defense Manpower Data Center, etc.) and DoS. We also incorporated follow-up interviews, phone calls, and fact-checking as we developed hypotheses to be tested by the survey.

These conversations yielded a preliminary assessment that the security priorities of armed contractors often conflicted with the counterinsurgency priorities of the military, which conflicted with the nation-building priorities of USAID and DoS. In particular, questions emerged regarding whether the immediate goals of the contractors were at odds with the broader foreign policy objectives of the U.S. government. Anecdotal evidence from these interviews implied that views on the usefulness or relative advantage of armed contractors were mixed, at best. In addition, many interviewees indicated that fighting a war and conducting nation-building at the same time and place was unprecedented, and the natural consequence would be a mixed set of objectives for DoD, DoS, and the PSCs. We sought to develop a survey to test these themes and hypotheses.

In addition, because our interviews revealed that the military and DoS perspectives were very different, we decided to conduct two separate surveys to compare and contrast the perspectives of employees from these different institutions. Because of the high value that this one-of-a-kind dataset would provide, RAND used its own internal funding to supplement the research so that a survey of DoS employees could be fielded and compared with the military survey. Because the two samples were treated as separate groups and were given slightly different survey questions, we discuss the survey methodology for each group separately.

Initial Research and Military Instrument Development

Based on the interviews and aforementioned research, a preliminary draft version of a survey instrument for military respondents was created in September 2006. Initial rounds of pretesting of the instrument were done via the recruitment of military fellows at the O4 to O6 levels currently serving in-house at RAND who had spent time in Iraq during OIF. These pretests helped not only to refine the question wording and concept capture of the study's primary hypotheses in question form but also to establish the appropriate target audience within our military population for the survey. It was determined that the most appropriate audience for the survey would be those personnel by pay grade category who would most likely have had direct working exposure to armed contractors while in the field. Based on these criteria, the pretest respondents recommended that the survey draw sample from pay grades E4 to E9, O2 to O6, and all warrant officers who had deployed as a part of Operation Iraqi Freedom.

As we investigated potential sources of military samples, we discovered another RAND project that was surveying a similar population group to address gaps in the existing literature concerning the prevalence and correlates of mental health conditions and traumatic brain injury stemming from military service in OEF and/or OIF. (The final findings of that project were published in *Invisible Wounds of War: Summary and Recommendations for Addressing Psychological and Cognitive Injuries*.[1]) Because that study had the advantage of substantially greater resources with which to build a broadly representative sample from scratch (and the sample was designed from the outset to continue as a panel for future surveys related to this particular population), an agreement was reached to stagger our survey to follow that one in time, so that we might draw the sample for our survey from those in that sample willing to participate in future research efforts.

Unlike with the Invisible Wounds study sample, no poststratification weighting was used in this opinion study of armed contractors. As this study's sample was drawn from the self-selected subset of the Invisible Wounds sample—those who completed the Invisible Wounds survey and agreed to possibly be recontacted for future surveys—and because a degree of nonresponse bias cannot be ruled out given that only 23 percent of those invited to participate completed the military version of the survey, its results cannot necessarily be expanded to the entire general population of military personnel deployed during OIF. Although we considered postweighting the military sample by

---

[1] *Invisible Wounds of War: Psychological and Cognitive Injuries, Their Consequences, and Services to Assist Recovery,* Terri Tanielian and Lisa H. Jaycox, eds., Santa Monica, Calif.: RAND, MG-720-CCF, 2008.

weighting responses by demographic variables, it was determined, because of the self-selected nature of those willing to participate in future studies, that this analytic strategy might potentially produce misleading results and thus was not implemented.

Given these factors, while it cannot be said that the results generalize to the overall population, the authors believe the greater value lies in the opinions of those people who worked closely with contractors: The results of this survey are presented primarily from that subset of respondents. These observations may now be used to guide further research and can inform more immediate shifts in policies related to the use of armed contractors in situations such as their engagement in OIF.

Military Sample Eligibility

The original sample (n = 953) for our survey of the military was drawn from the *Invisible Wounds* study participants based on the following eligibility criteria: time spent deployed in OIF (our study did not include those in the *Invisible Wounds* sample whose deployment experience encompassed OEF only); pay grades equaling E4 to E9, O2 to O6, and all warrant officers; and those who agreed at the conclusion of the *Invisible Wounds* survey to be contacted again for future RAND studies. The second, smaller sample group added from the *Invisible Wounds* sample database (n = 117) slightly after the initial fielding were "characteristically eligible" as military personnel who served in OIF, and were therefore qualified to participate in our opinion survey on armed contractors, although the *Invisible Wounds* study considered them to be "ineligible" for their survey because that study did not accept volunteers in their sampling approach. [2]

Informed Consent

Both the military and State Department surveys were approved and monitored by the RAND Institutional Review Board. The voluntary and confidential nature of the surveys prefaced both the military and State Department web surveys.

Survey of Military Personnel

The field plan for the military sample (n = 1,070) included an invitation email and a series of eight separate email reminders to sample members who had not yet completed their survey. Each email included an embedded link to the web survey and the

---

[2] "Volunteers" for the *Invisible Wounds* study came by way of someone directly recruited by email to be in the Invisible Wounds study (with a unique personal ID number) forwarding the message on to other military personnel in their address book who they knew to also have served in theater. These were primarily officers or high-end enlisted personnel, closely mirroring the eligible population for our armed contractors survey.

respondent's unique personal identification number (PIN). The emails were all signed by the RAND principal investigator with a reply-to address of the RAND survey team.

All respondents had the option to provide their contact information at the end of the survey if they wanted to receive a $10 incentive check. After 20 weeks in the field, we collected a total of 249 completed surveys (a 23.27 percent response rate.)

The respondents who did not submit a completed survey were categorized into one of five other final status codes at the end of the survey period. "Field Period Ended" cases are those for which the respondent neither completed any portion of the survey nor contacted RAND to opt out of the survey or indicate ineligibility. "Undeliverable" cases are those for which we received an automatically generated bounce-back message from an email we sent indicating that the email address was not viable. "Partial" cases are those in which the respondent completed some, but not all, of the survey questions online. "Ineligible" cases are those for which the respondent contacted RAND to indicate that he or she did not have enough experience working with armed contractors to complete the survey and/or had not served in theater in Iraq. Finally, "refused" cases are those for which the respondent contacted RAND to refuse participation in the survey. The breakdown of all final outcomes for the military sample is displayed in Table A.1.

Table A.1
Final Outcomes for Military Sample

Final Status	Number	Percentage of Sample
Field period ended	578	54.02
Complete	249	23.27
Undeliverable	216	20.18
Partial	15	1.40
Ineligible	7	0.65
Refused	5	0.46

Participant Demographics

Note that in the following tables, some totals do not sum to 100 percent because of rounding.

Q1: What branch of service have you been in most recently?				
	Frequency	Percentage	Cumulative Frequency	Cumulative Percentage
Army	151	60.89	151	60.89
Navy	27	10.89	178	71.77
Air Force	30	12.10	208	83.87
Marine Corps	40	16.13	248	100.00

Frequency Missing = 1

Q2: Still in military?

	Frequency	Percentage	Cumulative Frequency	Cumulative Percentage
Active Service	144	57.83	144	57.83
Guard/Reserve—currently activated/full time	23	9.24	167	67.07
Guard/Reserve—traditional/part time	28	11.24	195	78.31
Separated from service	54	21.69	249	100.00

Q3: If separated from service—Current status in the military

	Frequency	Percentage	Cumulative Frequency	Cumulative Percentage
Retired	32	59.26	32	59.26
Discharged with severance or military disability payments	9	16.67	41	75.93
Discharged without severance or payment	10	18.52	51	94.44
Other (please specify):	3	5.56	54	100.00

Frequency Missing = 195

Q4: Highest pay grade achieved

	Frequency	Percentage	Cumulative Frequency	Cumulative Percentage
E1–E5	85	34.55	85	34.55
E6–E9, W2–W4	101	41.06	186	75.61
O1–O3	20	8.13	206	83.74
O4–O6	40	16.26	246	100.00

Frequency Missing = 3

State Department Sampling and Eligibility

Because of our preliminary assessments that the DoD and DoS would yield very different perspectives about the roles, benefits, drawbacks, and implications of widespread use of PSCs, we sought to include a second survey of DoS personnel that could be used in comparison with the military survey. Permission to develop such a survey in collaboration with DoS was initially sought in 2006 and was granted in 2008. We worked with assistant secretaries in the Bureau of Resource Management and Administration offices, and the Under Secretary for Management, to develop the survey.

The study was endorsed by DoS's Under Secretary for Management and Acting Assistant Secretary for Diplomatic Security, and approved for distribution by the Near East Asia Bureau, which controls the recruitment and deployment of personnel to Iraq.

The State Department sample was assembled by State from the following sources:

- DoS employee list
- OGA list (assembled from training records at the Foreign Service Institute)
- 3161s (those with one-year limited Civil Service appointments).

The final State Department instrument contained more than 50 differences from the military version of the instrument. The full survey contained 23 separate web survey screens and 58 survey items.

Survey of State Department Personnel

The field plan for the State Department sample was much like the field plan for the military sample but was condensed into a shorter timeline and benefited from the active support of the survey by the State Department (coordinated through its Diplomatic Security division). Prior to the official email invitation being sent to the sample by RAND to invite participation in the study, the division chief for Diplomatic Security emailed a note of support for the survey to the entire sample and encouraged their participation. Later that day, an invitation email was sent to all sample members and a series of four separate reminder emails was sent to sample members who had not yet completed their survey. Like the military sample, each email to the State Department sample included an embedded link to the web survey and the respondent's unique PIN. The emails were all signed by the RAND Principal Investigator with a reply-to address of the RAND survey team.

The invitation emails were sent on October 15, 2008, to 1,727 recipients. Four reminder emails were sent about a week apart.

After 33 days in the field, we collected a total of 834 completed surveys (48.29 percent), and 58 partially completed surveys (3.36 percent), from which we were still able to utilize the data. Thus 892 participants' responses were included in the final dataset (a 51.65 percent response rate).

As with the military sample, the respondents in the State Department sample who did not submit a completed survey were categorized into one of five other final status codes at the end of the survey period. The categories are the same as described in the section about the military sample. The breakdown of all final outcomes for the State Department sample is displayed in Table A.2.

Table A.2
Final Outcomes for State Department Sample

Final Status	Number	Percentage of Sample
Complete	834	48.29
Field period ended	541	31.23
Undeliverable	239	13.83
Partial	58	3.36
Ineligible	29	1.67
Refused	17	0.98

Participant Characteristics

Q2: What is the highest pay grade you achieved with the State Department?

	Frequency	Percentage	Cumulative Frequency	Cumulative Percentage
FE-CM	3	0.35	3	0.35
FE-MC	24	2.78	27	3.13
FE-OC	43	4.99	70	8.12
FS-1	92	10.67	162	18.79
FS-2	152	17.63	314	36.43
FS-3	214	24.83	528	61.25
FS-4	73	8.47	601	69.72
FS-5	17	1.97	618	71.69
FS-6	8	0.93	626	72.62
GS-1	1	0.12	627	72.74
GS-3	2	0.23	629	72.97
GS-5	1	0.12	630	73.09
GS-6	1	0.12	631	73.20
GS-10	1	0.12	632	73.32
GS-11	6	0.70	638	74.01
GS-12	9	1.04	647	75.06
GS-13	25	2.90	672	77.96
GS-14	37	4.29	709	82.25
GS-15	64	7.42	773	89.68
SES-I	9	1.04	782	90.72
SES-II	2	0.23	784	90.95
SES-III	1	0.12	785	91.07
SES-IV	2	0.23	787	91.30
SES-V	1	0.12	788	91.42
3161-I	2	0.23	790	91.65
3161-II	6	0.70	796	92.34
3161-III	14	1.62	810	93.97
3161-IV	24	2.78	834	96.75
3161-V	28	3.25	862	100.00

Frequency Missing = 30

Q3: What cone or specialty have you worked with most recently?				
	Frequency	Percentage	Cumulative Frequency	Cumulative Percentage
Generalist—Political Affairs	152	19.14	152	19.14
Generalist—Economic Affairs	70	8.82	222	27.96
Generalist—Consular Affairs	43	5.42	265	33.38
Generalist—Management Affairs	55	6.93	320	40.30
Generalist—Public Diplomacy	62	7.81	382	48.11
Specialist—Security	168	21.16	550	69.27
Specialist—Administration	36	4.53	586	73.80
Specialist—Construction and Engineering	15	1.89	601	75.69
Specialist—Office Management Specialist	32	4.03	633	79.72
Specialist—Information Technology	66	8.31	699	88.04
Specialist—Medical and Health	13	1.64	712	89.67
N/A—not in either cone/specialty	82	10.33	794	100.00

Frequency Missing = 98

Statistical Analysis Methods

Weighting and Generalizability of Results

All statistical analyses were performed unweighted. While the respondents to our military survey were a subset of respondents to the Invisible Wounds survey, using the weights developed by that project was precluded by privacy considerations, as well as by the self-selection of our survey sample, which made weighting to the general military population problematic. For the State Department survey respondents, we did not know of any accessible data on the distribution of demographic characteristics in the general population of diplomats with OIF assignments. Thus, we also elected not to develop poststratification weights for the State Department respondents. The DoS sample, however, was also in essence a census of all State employees and contractors (minus those 3,161 contractors who requested that the State Department not include their contact information in the sample list passed to RAND). This, combined with the high response rate achieved for the DoS survey, provides a greater case for generalizability of the findings than does the military survey.

Data Analysis Methods

We first performed separate analyses on the military and State Department datasets to assess the degree to which demographic characteristics of each group were associated with the distributions of answers to survey questions regarding their perceptions of armed contractors.

Military Data

For the military data, we produced two-way contingency tables for all pairings of nine demographic characteristics of interest with 29 survey questions about armed contractors. The demographics were frequency of interaction with armed contractors, whether the respondent was still in the military at the time of the survey, pay grade (stratified by enlisted military versus officers), number of OIF deployments, year of return from the most recent OIF deployment (for those with exactly one OIF deployment), education, race/ethnicity, age, and gender.

With the exception of binary gender, these demographics were collected as polytomous categorical variables or continuous variables on the military survey. Due to the small sample size of military survey respondents (n = 249 in the final dataset), we dichotomized the demographics based on their distributions in the raw data to create 2×2 and 2×5 contingency tables (depending on the number of response categories for armed contractor questions). For survey questions with a response choice of "No Opinion," we excluded respondents who marked "No Opinion" from our analysis.

We performed Pearson Chi-square tests on the contingency tables discussed above to test the null hypothesis of independence of demographics and perceptions of armed contractors. Despite aggregating the demographic characteristics into two categories each, more than 20 percent of cells in some contingency tables had expected cell counts of less than five. For these sparsely populated tables, the Pearson Chi-square test is inappropriate due to its reliance on asymptotic results. Therefore, we used Fisher's exact test in these cases. Fisher's exact test is appropriate for testing independence in contingency tables with small total sample sizes and/or small expected cell counts. The p-values from Pearson's Chi-square test and Fisher's exact test are not directly comparable, so results of the two different tests must be evaluated with caution. When p-values are reported in the text hereafter, they refer to Pearson's Chi-square test unless otherwise noted.

After completing the analysis described above using data from all respondents to the military survey (n = 249), we repeated the analysis using only the subset of respondents (n = 152, 61 percent of data) who marked "Sometimes" or "Often" for question 6 on the military survey ("During OIF, how often did you interact with armed contractors hired either directly or indirectly by the U.S. government?").

State Department Data

We examined the responses to the State Department survey (n = 892, 834 completed + 58 partially completed surveys) in a manner analogous to the military data analysis. Several demographic characteristics were the same as those used in the military analysis: frequency of interaction with armed contractors, pay grade (stratified by FS versus GS classification), number of OIF assignments, year of return from the most recent OIF assignment (for those with exactly one OIF assignment), education, race/ethnicity, age, and gender. Additional demographic characteristics included job specialty or cone (stratified by generalists versus specialists) and whether the respondent had served in the U.S. military. As with the military analysis, we dichotomized the demographics based on their distributions in the raw data.

We produced contingency tables and Pearson Chi-square tests (or Fisher's exact tests when necessary) for all pairwise crosses of the State Department demographic characteristics with 37 questions regarding perceptions of armed contractors. As with the military analysis, we performed these tests both on the full dataset (n = 892) and the subset of respondents who interacted "Sometimes" or "Often" with armed contractors (n = 807, 90 percent of respondents).

Military/State Department Comparisons

After analyzing the military and State Department survey data separately, we compared the response patterns of the two groups in which the same question appeared on both surveys (26 items). Communications with the State Department indicated that the experiences of diplomats vary considerably by their membership in the FS, GS, or 3161 categories. Furthermore, they suggested dichotomizing the FS and FS groups as follows: FS-2 and below versus FS-1 and above; GS-14 and below versus GS-15 and above. Furthermore, military officers tend to be more similar to State Department personnel than enlisted military in terms of level of responsibility. For these reasons we stratified the State Department respondents into five groups (FS-2 and below, n = 464; FS-1 and above, n = 162; GS-14 and below, n = 83; GS-15 and above, n = 79; 3161's, n = 74) and compared each group to military officers (n = 60) separately.

For each of the 26 common survey items we performed Pearson's Chi-square test for independence of the distribution of responses for a given State Department subgroup and military officers. When contingency tables were sparse, we used Fisher's exact test (noted in the discussion of results where applicable). As with the separate analyses of the two datasets, we repeated this analysis subsetting on respondents with more frequent interaction with armed contractors ("Sometimes" or "Often"). Sample sizes for this subset were as follows: military officers, n = 38; FS-2 and below, n = 436; FS-1 and above, n = 150; GS-14 and below, n = 76; GS-15 and above, n = 64; 3161s, N = 67.

APPENDIX B

Screen Shots of Final Survey as Fielded to Members of the Military

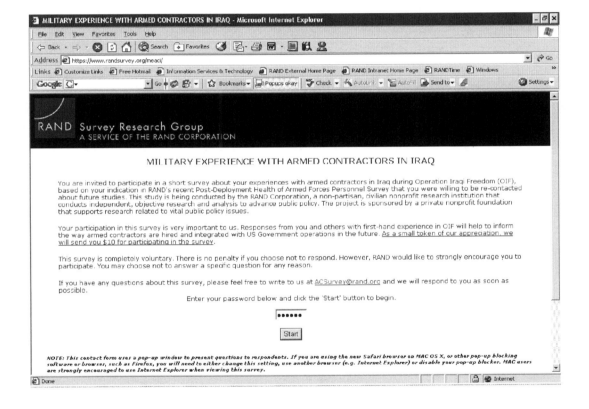

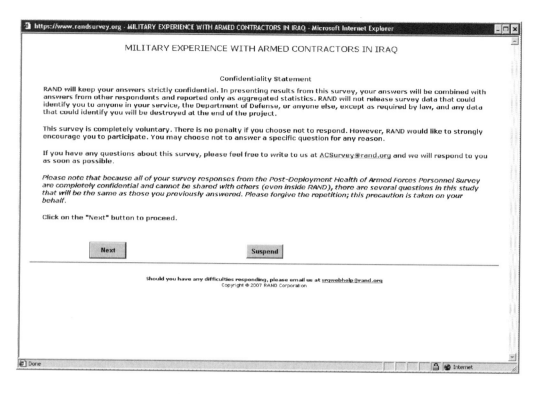

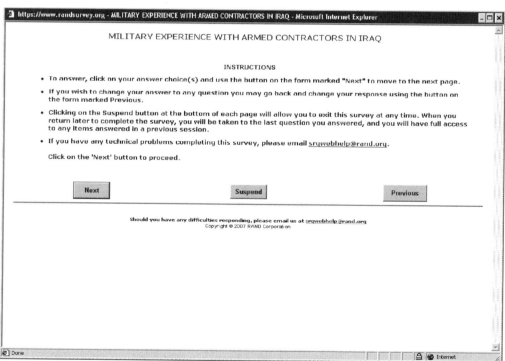

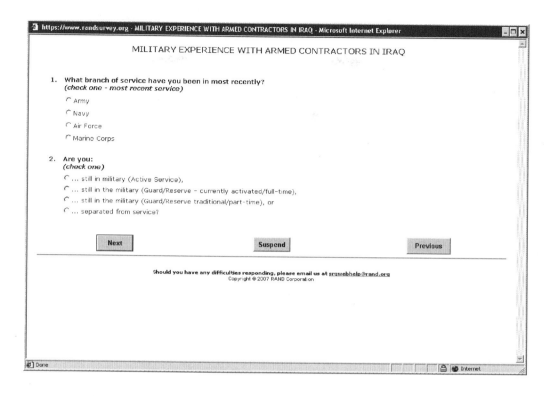

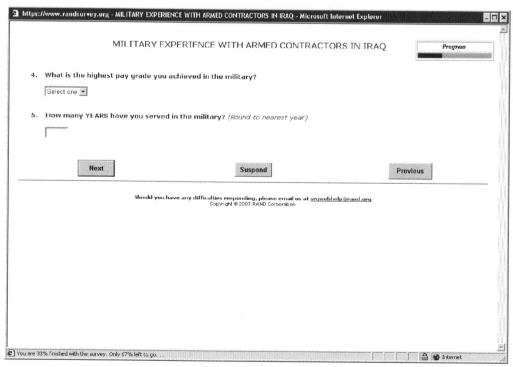

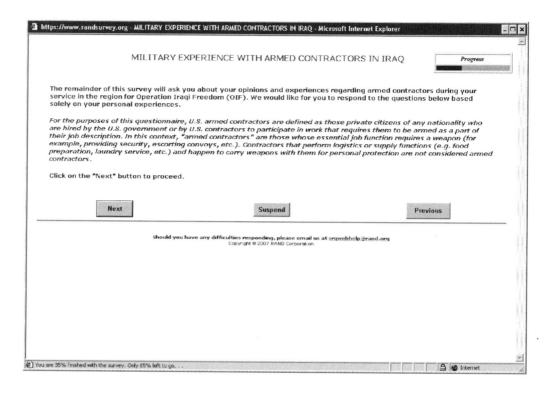

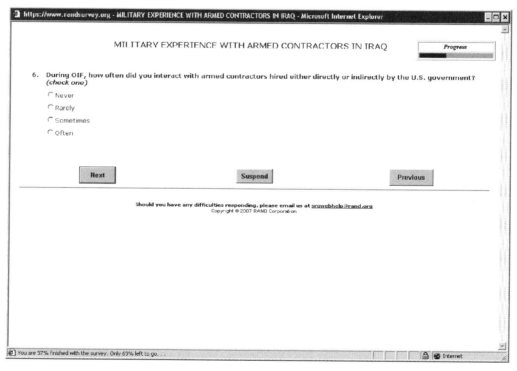

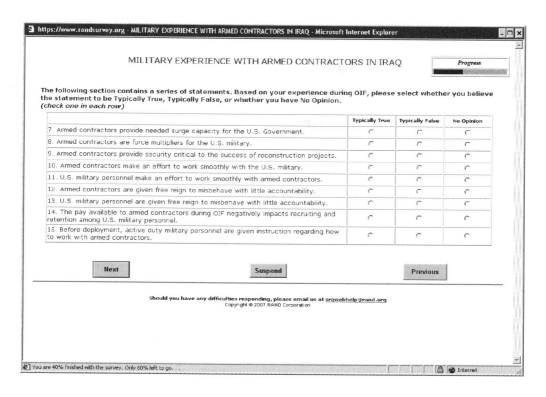

MILITARY EXPERIENCE WITH ARMED CONTRACTORS IN IRAQ

The following section contains a series of statements. Based on your experience during OIF, please select whether you believe the statement to be Typically True, Typically False, or whether you have No Opinion. *(check one in each row)*

	Typically True	Typically False	No Opinion
7. Armed contractors provide needed surge capacity for the U.S. Government.	○	○	○
8. Armed contractors are force multipliers for the U.S. military.	○	○	○
9. Armed contractors provide security critical to the success of reconstruction projects.	○	○	○
10. Armed contractors make an effort to work smoothly with the U.S. military.	○	○	○
11. U.S. military personnel make an effort to work smoothly with armed contractors.	○	○	○
12. Armed contractors are given free reign to misbehave with little accountability.	○	○	○
13. U.S. military personnel are given free reign to misbehave with little accountability.	○	○	○
14. The pay available to armed contractors during OIF negatively impacts recruiting and retention among U.S. military personnel.	○	○	○
15. Before deployment, active duty military personnel are given instruction regarding how to work with armed contractors.	○	○	○

Next   Suspend   Previous

Should you have any difficulties responding, please email us at srqwebhelp@rand.org
Copyright © 2007 RAND Corporation

You are 40% finished with the survey. Only 60% left to go. . .

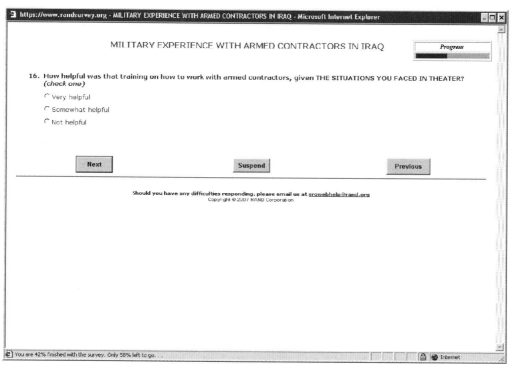

MILITARY EXPERIENCE WITH ARMED CONTRACTORS IN IRAQ

16. **How helpful was that training on how to work with armed contractors, given THE SITUATIONS YOU FACED IN THEATER?** *(check one)*

   ○ Very helpful
   ○ Somewhat helpful
   ○ Not helpful

Next   Suspend   Previous

Should you have any difficulties responding, please email us at srqwebhelp@rand.org
Copyright © 2007 RAND Corporation

You are 42% finished with the survey. Only 58% left to go. . .

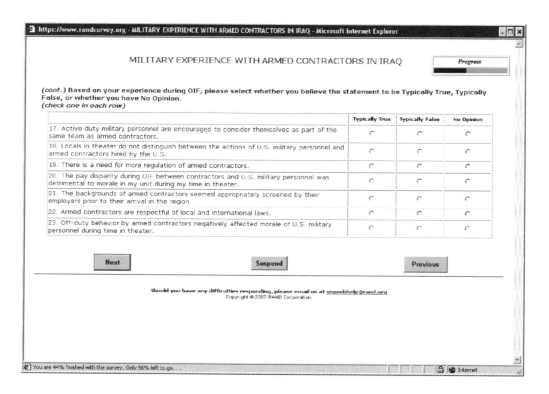

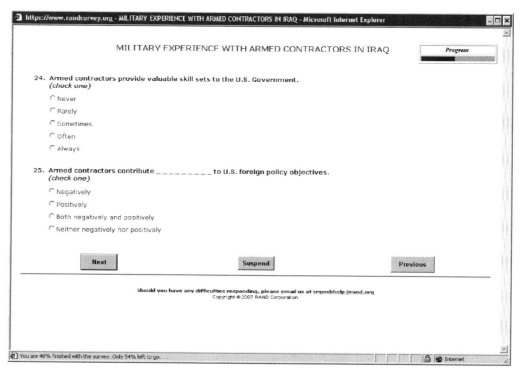

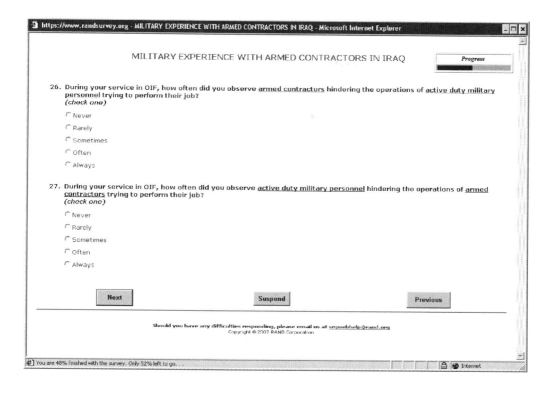

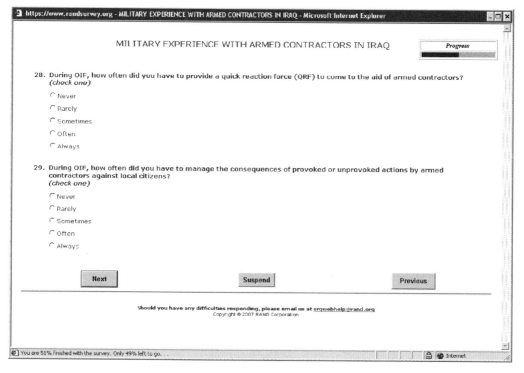

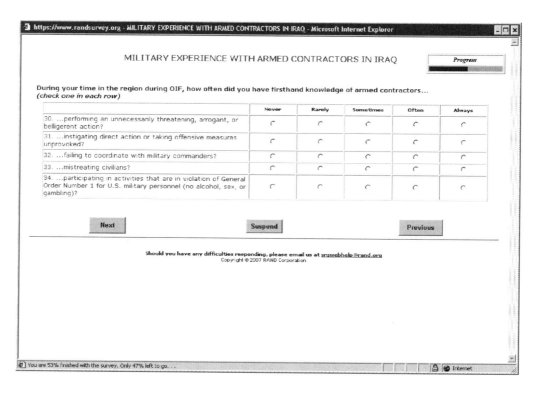

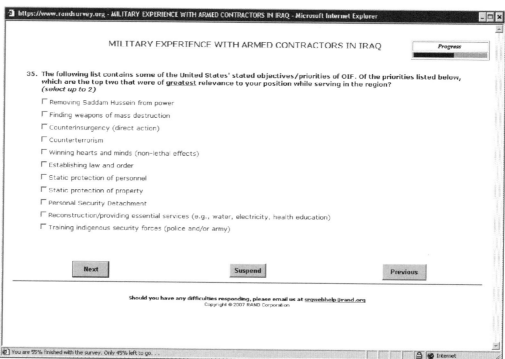

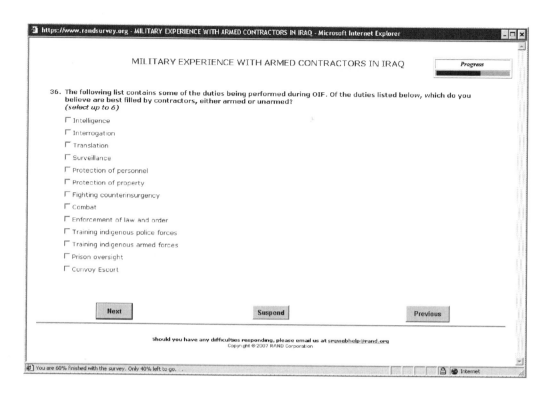

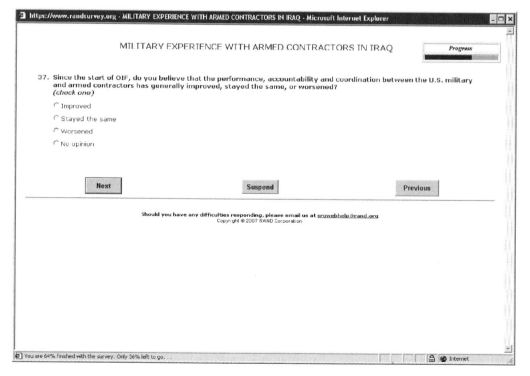

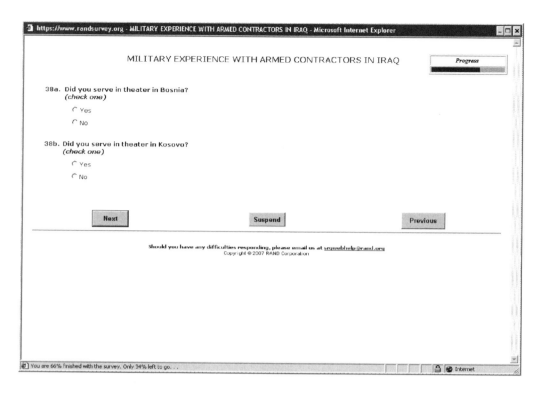

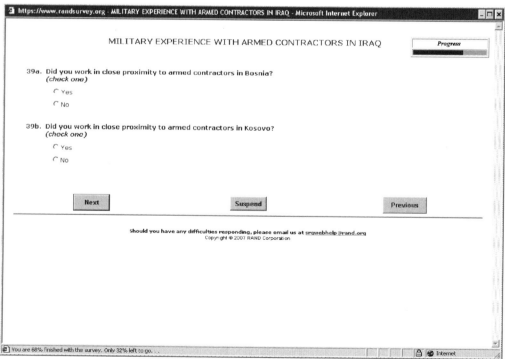

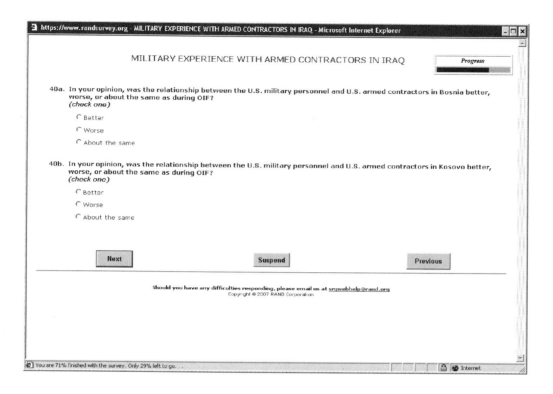

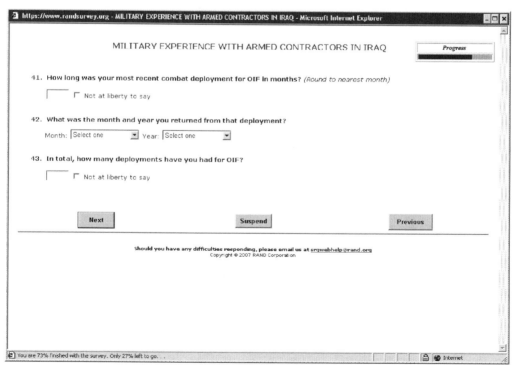

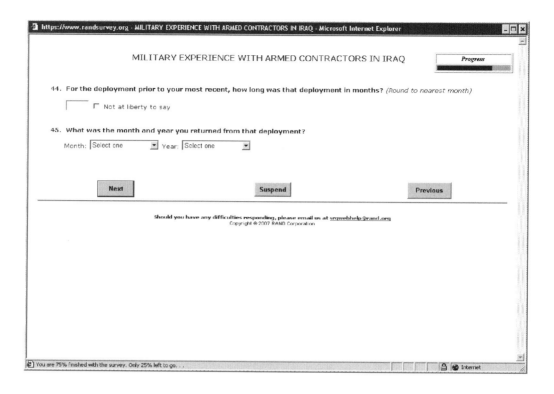

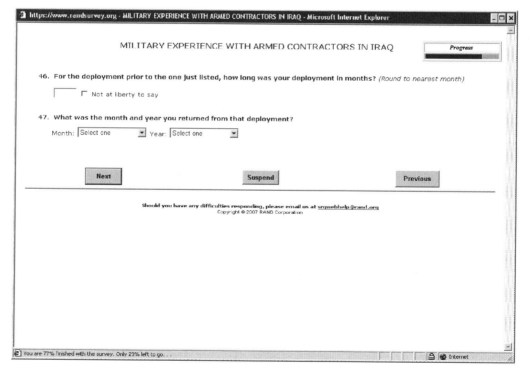

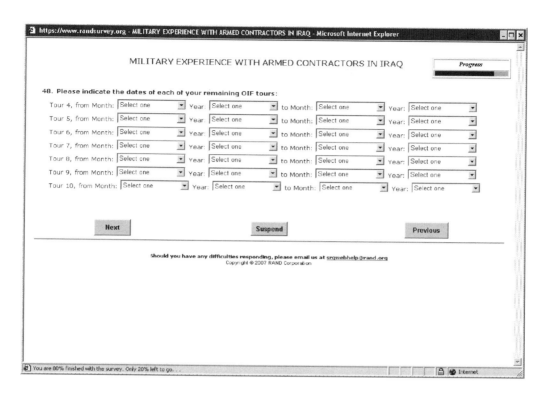

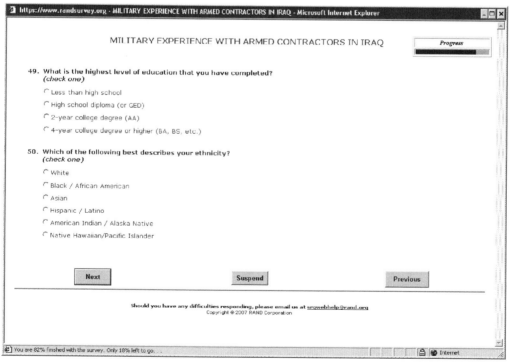

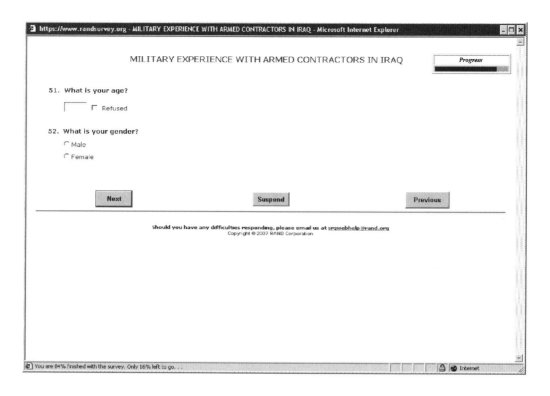

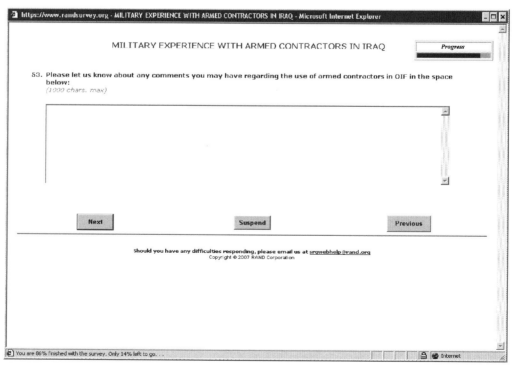

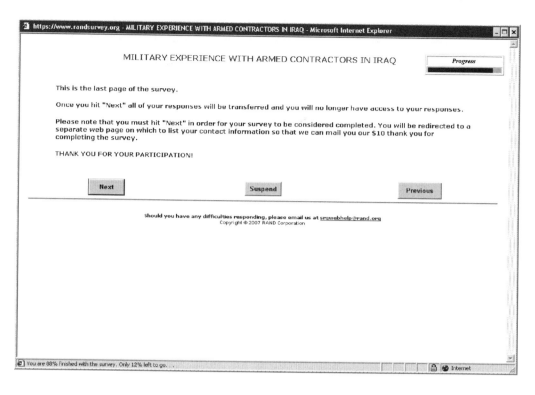

MILITARY EXPERIENCE WITH ARMED CONTRACTORS IN IRAQ

This is the last page of the survey.

Once you hit "Next" all of your responses will be transferred and you will no longer have access to your responses.

Please note that you must hit "Next" in order for your survey to be considered completed. You will be redirected to a separate web page on which to list your contact information so that we can mail you our $10 thank you for completing the survey.

THANK YOU FOR YOUR PARTICIPATION!

Next   Suspend   Previous

Should you have any difficulties responding, please email us at srqwebhelp@rand.org
Copyright © 2007 RAND Corporation

You are 88% finished with the survey. Only 12% left to go. . .

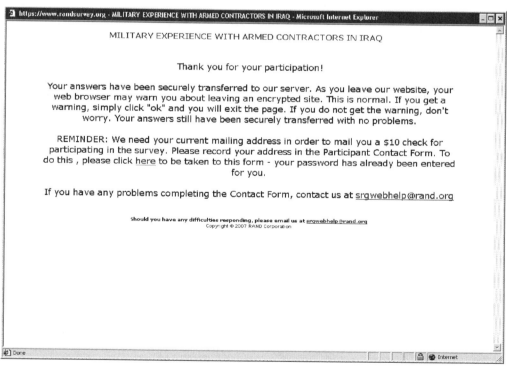

MILITARY EXPERIENCE WITH ARMED CONTRACTORS IN IRAQ

Thank you for your participation!

Your answers have been securely transferred to our server. As you leave our website, your web browser may warn you about leaving an encrypted site. This is normal. If you get a warning, simply click "ok" and you will exit the page. If you do not get the warning, don't worry. Your answers still have been securely transferred with no problems.

REMINDER: We need your current mailing address in order to mail you a $10 check for participating in the survey. Please record your address in the Participant Contact Form. To do this , please click here to be taken to this form - your password has already been entered for you.

If you have any problems completing the Contact Form, contact us at srqwebhelp@rand.org

Should you have any difficulties responding, please email us at srqwebhelp@rand.org
Copyright © 2007 RAND Corporation

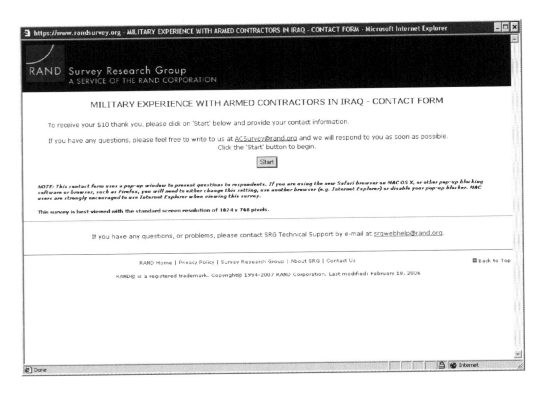

Please provide us with your name, address, and phone if you wish to be mailed $10 once this survey is received as a thank you for your participation. If you would like a copy of the results sent to you at the end of the study, please provide your e-mail address.

Name:

Street Address:

City:

State:

Zip:

Phone: (   )   -   Ext.

Email:

Thank you for participating in this important survey. If you have provided your e-mail address above, a link to the study's results will be e-mailed to you once the study is completed.

Please note that you must hit "Next" in order for this Contact Form to be considered completed.

THANK YOU FOR YOUR PARTICIPATION!

Next

Should you have any difficulties responding, please email us at srqwebhelp@rand.org
Copyright © 2007 RAND Corporation

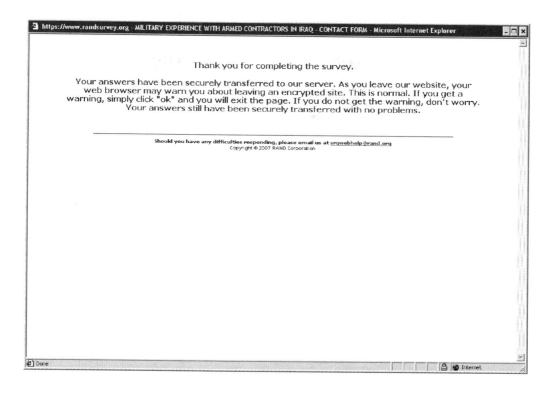

APPENDIX C

Screen Shots of Final Survey as Fielded to State Department Personnel

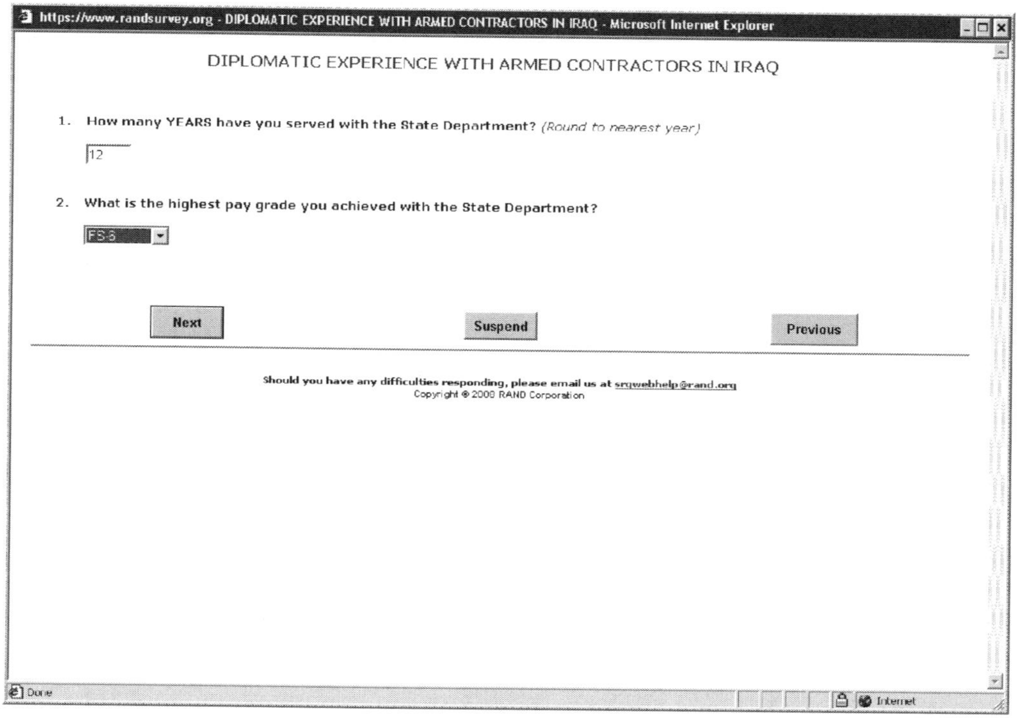
https://www.randsurvey.org - DIPLOMATIC EXPERIENCE WITH ARMED CONTRACTORS IN IRAQ - Microsoft Internet Explorer
DIPLOMATIC EXPERIENCE WITH ARMED CONTRACTORS IN IRAQ
1. How many YEARS have you served with the State Department? (Round to nearest year)
12
2. What is the highest pay grade you achieved with the State Department?
FS-3
Next
Suspend
Previous
Should you have any difficulties responding, please email us at srqwebhelp@rand.org
Copyright © 2008 RAND Corporation
Done
Internet

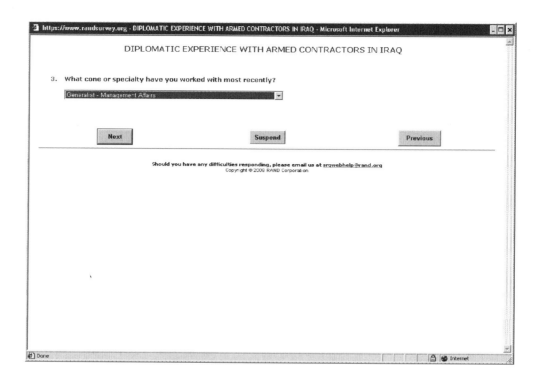

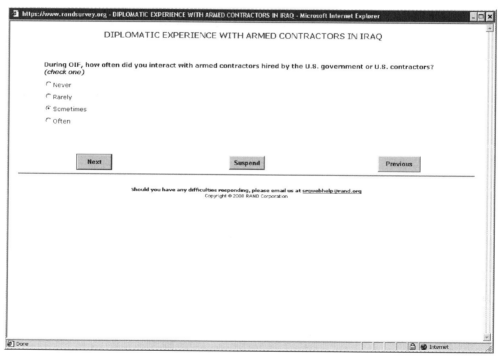

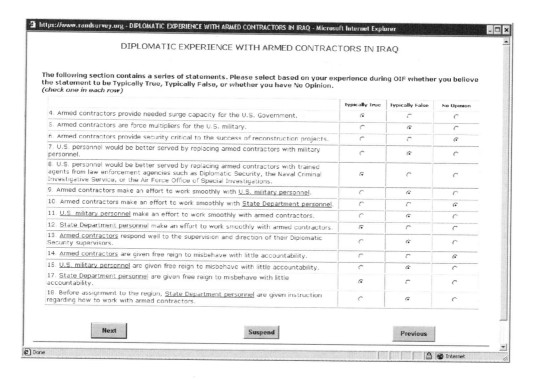

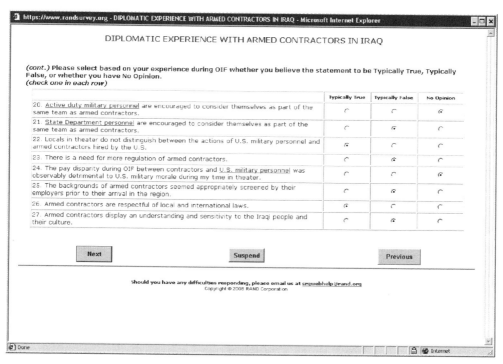

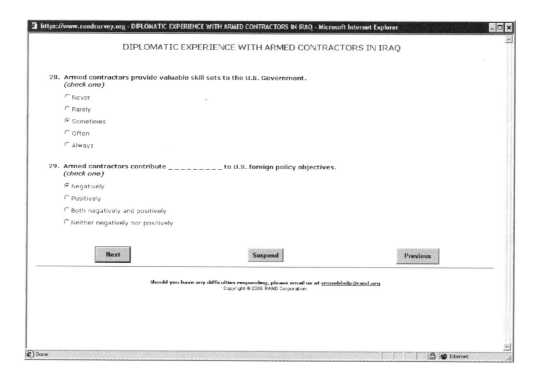

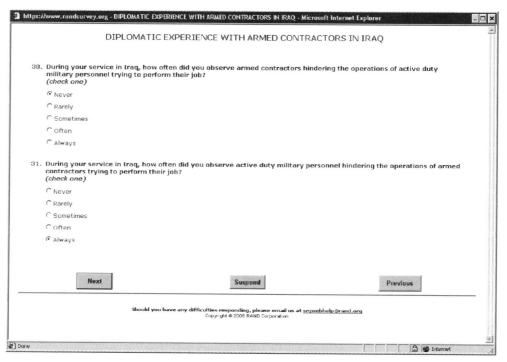

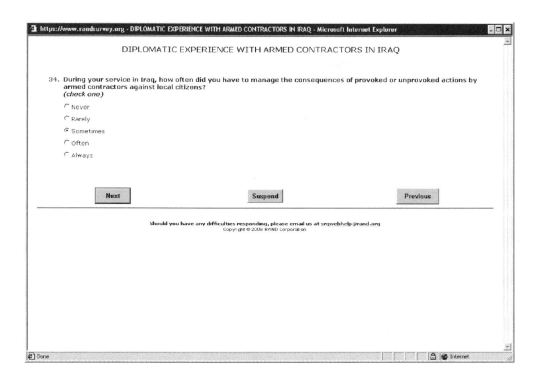

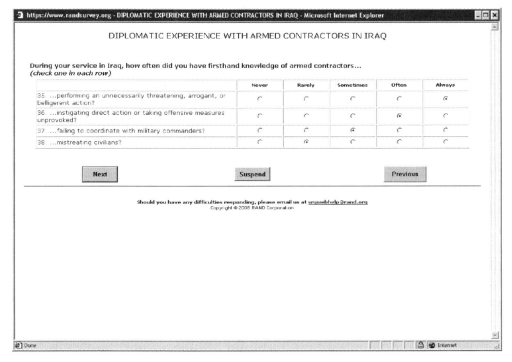

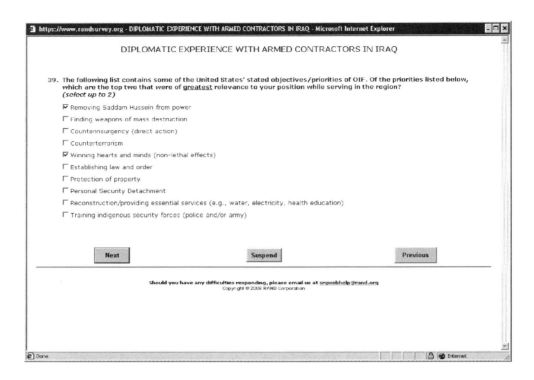

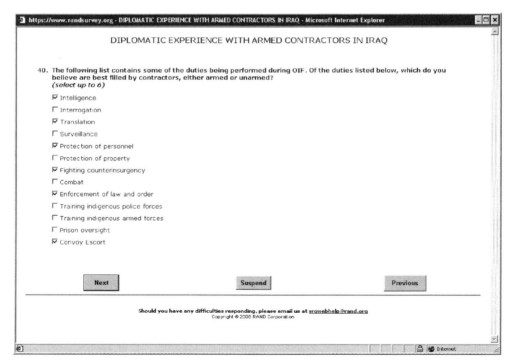

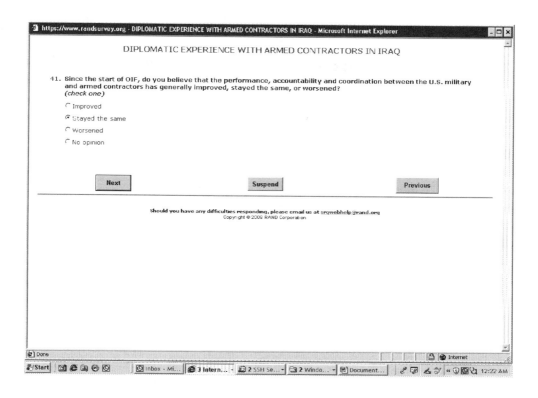

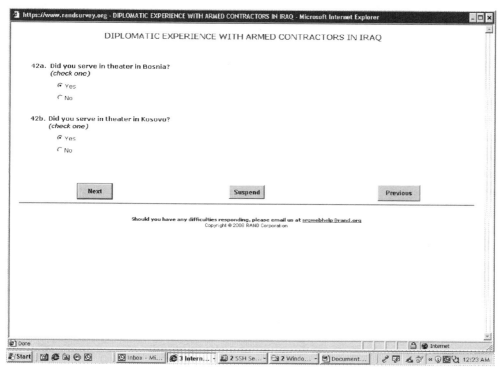

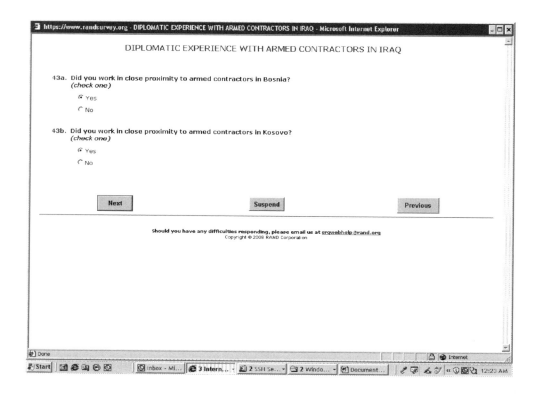

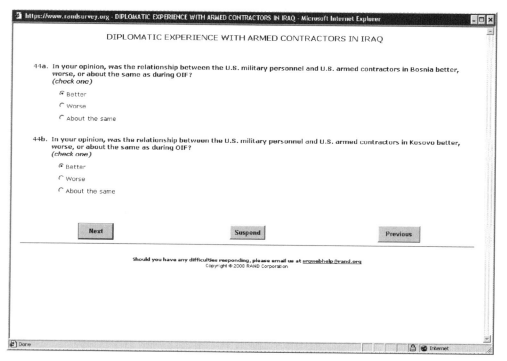

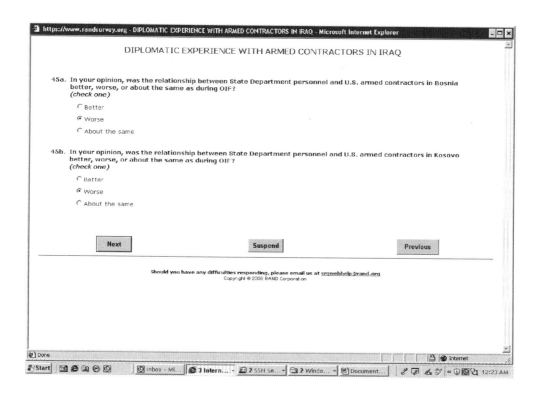

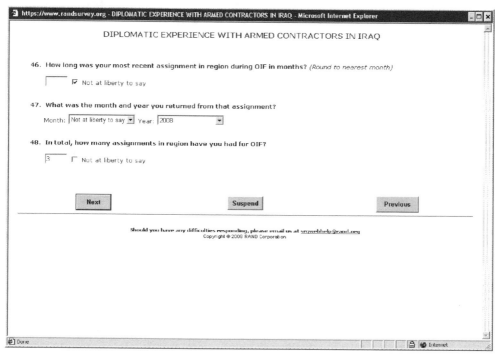

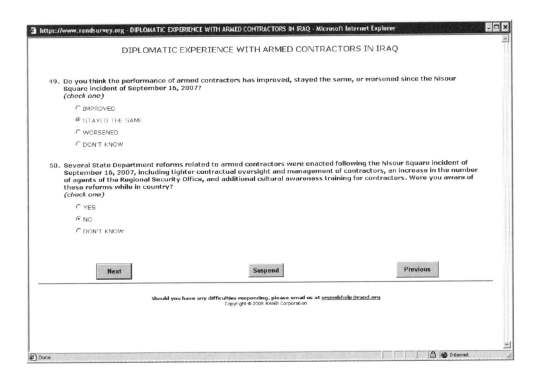

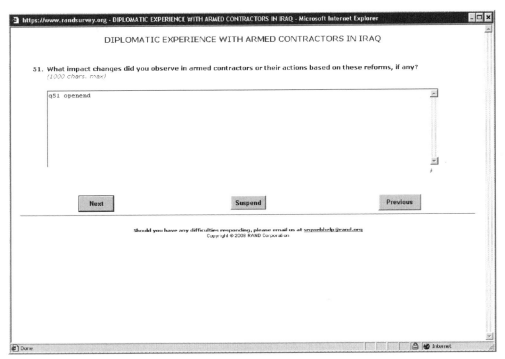

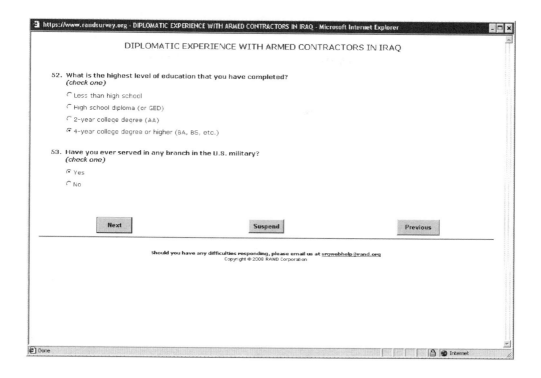

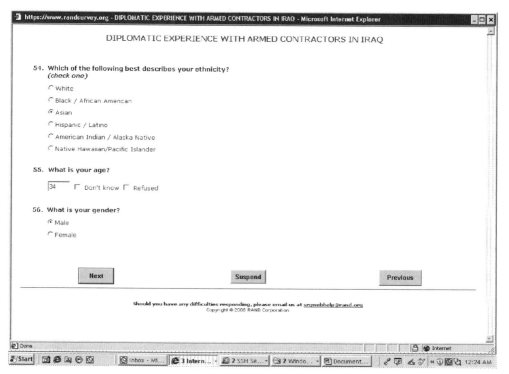

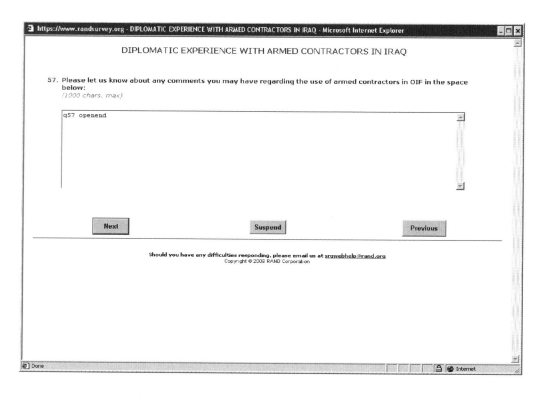

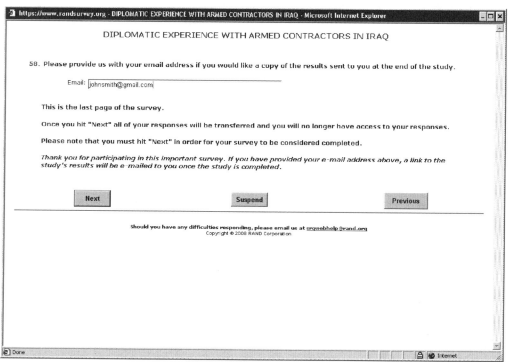

References

Adams, Thomas. (1999) "The Mercenaries and the Privatization of Conflict." *Parameters*, 103–116.

Agreement Between the United States of American and the Republic of Iraq on the Withdrawal of United States Forces From Iraq and the Organization of Their Activities during Their Temporary Presence in Iraq. (2009) Article 12.

"A New Legal Framework for Military Contractors?" As of October 15, 2007: http://lapa.princeton.edu/conferences/military07/MilCon_Workshop_Summary.pdf

Associated Press. (28 September 2007) "Blackwater Blamed for Fallujah Bloodshed." *Newser.*

Avant, Deborah D. (2005) *The Market for Force: The Consequences of Privatizing Security.* New York: Cambridge University Press.

Bianco, Anthony, and Stephanie Anderson Forest. (15 September 2003) "Outsourcing War an Inside Look at Brown & Root, the Kingpin of Americas New Military-Industrial Complex." *Business Week.*

Bowmen, Marion. (2007) "Privatizing While Transforming." *Defense Horizons, 57.*

Broder, John M., and David Johnston. (31 October 2007) "U.S. Military Will Supervise Security Firms." *New York Times* A1.

Brookings Institution. (May 2003, May 2004, May 2005, April 2006). "Iraq Index: Tracking Reconstruction and Security in Post-Saddam Iraq."

Brooks, Doug. (2000) "Messiahs or Mercenaries? The Future of International Private Military Services." *International Peacekeeping* 7: 120–144.

Burns, John. (2007) "The Deadly Game of Private Security." *New York Times*, 23 September, 1.

Cameron, Lindsey. (September 2006) "Private Military Companies: Their Status Under International Humanitarian Law and Its Impact on Their Regulation." *ICRC Review* 88, 863.

Campbell, Gordon. (2000) "Contractors on the Battlefield: The Ethics of Paying Civilians to Enter Harm's Way and Requiring Soldiers to Depend Upon Them." *Joint Services Conference on Professional Ethics 2000.* Springfield, Va.

Carafano, James Jay. (2008) *Private Sector, Public Wars: Contractors in Combat— Afghanistan, Iraq, and Future Conflicts (The Changing Face of War).* Westport, Conn.: Praeger Security International.

CBS News. (20 November 2008) "U.S. Contractors Lose Immunity in Iraq Security Deal. "

Clark, Martha K. (2008) *In The Company of Soldiers: Private Security Companies' Impact on Military Effectiveness and the Democratic Advantage.* Ithaca, N.Y.: Cornell University, doctoral dissertation.

Cohen, William. (1997) *Defense Reform Initiative Report.* Washington, D.C.: Department of Defense.

Coker, Christopher. (1999) "Outsourcing War." *Cambridge Review of International Affairs* 13: 95–113.

Commission on Wartime Contracting in Iraq and Afghanistan. (2009) *At What Cost? Contingency Contracting in Iraq and Afghanistan: Interim Report.*

Committee on Armed Services. (2007) Nominations Before the Senates Armed Service Committee. Committee on Armed Services. 1st Session, 110th Congress, Washington, D.C.: Government Printing Office.

Committee on Foreign Affairs. (2002) *Ninth Report of the Foreign Affairs Committee: Private Military Companies.* London: British Parliament.

Committee on Government Reform. (2006) *Private Security Firm Standards, Cooperation and Coordination on the Battlefield.* Washington, D.C.

Committee on Oversight and Government Reform. (2007a) *Hearing on Blackwater USA.* Washington, D.C.

_____. (2007b) *Private Military Contractors in Iraq: An Examination of Blackwater's Actions in Fallujah.* Washington, D.C.

Congressional Budget Office. (2005) *Logistics Support for Deployed Military Forces.* Washington, D.C.

_____. (2008) *Contractors' Support of U.S. Operations in Iraq.* Washington, D.C.

Cottier, Michael. (2006) "Elements for Contracting and Regulating Private Security and Military Companies." *ICRC Review* 88, September, 863.

Defense Science Board. (1996) *Report of the Defense Science Board Task Force on Outsourcing and Privatization.*

Department of the Army. (1985) Army Regulation (AR) 700-137, "Logistics Civil Augmentation Program." Washington, D.C.

_____. (1999) Field Manual (FM) 3-100.31, "Contracting Support in the Battlefield." Washington, D.C.

Department of Defense. (1990) "Continuation of Essential DoD Contractor Services During Crises," DoD Instruction No. 3020.37.

_____. (2001) *Quadrennial Defense Review Report.* Washington, D.C.

_____. (2007) *Management of DoD Contractors and Contractor Personnel Accompanying U.S. Armed Forces in Contingency Operations Outside the United States.* Washington, D.C.

Department of Defense and Department of State. (2007) *Memorandum on the Use of Private Security Contractors,* Washington, D.C.

Donahue, John D. (1989) *The Privatization Decision: Public Ends, Private Means.* New York: Basic Books.

Donald, Dominick. (2006) "After the Bubble: British Private Security Companies after Iraq." Whitehall Paper 66. London: RUSI.

Dowling, Maria, and Vincent Feck. (1999) "Feasibility of Joint Engineering and Logistics Contracts." Maxwell Air Force Base: Air Command Staff College, Wright Flyer Paper No. 7.

Duginski, Paul. (4 July 2007) "Private Contractors Outnumber U.S. Troops in Iraq." *Los Angeles Times.*

Elsea, Jennifer K., Moshe Schwartz, and Kennon H. Nakamura. (2008) *Private Security Contractors in Iraq: Background, Legal Status, and Other Issues.* CRS Report for Congress. Washington, D.C.: Congressional Research Service.

Ezell, Virginia H. (1999) "Logisticians and Contractors Team for Logcap Exercise." *Army Logistician* 31: 16–17.

Fainaru, Steve. (15 April 2007a) "Four Hired Guns in an Armored Truck, Bullets Flying, and a Pickup and a Taxi Brought to a Halt. Who Did the Shooting and Why?" *Washington Post*, A01.

_____. (16 June 2007b) "Iraq Contractors Face Growing Parallel War; as Security Work Increases, So Do Casualties." *Washington Post*, A01.

_____. (12 August 2007c) "U.S. Pays Millions in Cost Overruns for Security in Iraq." *Washington Post*, A01.

_____. (24 December 2007d) "Warnings Unheeded on Guards in Iraq; Despite Shootings, Security Companies Expanded Presence." *Washington Post*, A01.

_____. (2008) *Big Boy Rules: America's Mercenaries Fighting in Iraq*. Cambridge, Mass.: Da Capo Press.

Fredland, Eric. (2004) "Outsourcing Military Force: A Transactions Cost Perspective on the Role of Military Companies." *Defence and Peace Economics* 15: 205–219.

Friedman, Robert. (2002) "Civilian Contractors on the Battlefield: A Partnership with Commercial Industry or a Recipe for Failure?" Carlisle Barracks, Pa.: U.S. Army War College.

GAO—*See* Government Accountability Office.

Garcia-Perez, Isolde. (1999) "Contractors on the Battlefield in the 21st Century." *Army Logistician* 21: 40–44.

General Assembly. (2007) *Use of Mercenaries as a Means of Violating Human Rights and Impeding the Exercise of the Right of Peoples to Self-Determination*. New York: United Nations.

Gillert, Douglas J. (10 April 1996) "DoD Looks to Outsourcing to Improve Combat Edge." *American Forces Press Service*.

Glanz, James, (29 October 2008) "Report on Iraq Security Lists 310 Contractors, from U.S. To Uganda." *New York Times*, 5.

Glanz, James, and Alissa J. Rubin. (2 October 2007a) "From Errand to Fatal Shot to Hail of Fire to 17 Deaths." *New York Times*.

_____. (8 October 2007b) "Blackwater Shootings 'Murder,' Iraq Says." *New York Times*.

Government Accountability Office. (1981) *Civil Servants and Contract Employees: Who Should Do What for the Federal Government?* Report to the Congress. Washington, D.C.

_____. (2000) *DoD Competitive Sourcing: Some Progress but Continuing Challenges Remain in Meeting Program Goals*. Washington, D.C.

_____. (2003a) *Defense Management: DoD Faces Challenges Implementing Its Core Competency Approach and A-76 Competitions*. Washington, D.C.

_____. (2003b) *Military Operations Contractors Provide Vital Service to Deployed Forces but Are Not Adequately Addressed in DoD Plans*. Washington, D.C.

_____. (2005) *Rebuilding Iraq: Actions Needed to Improve Use of Private Security Providers*. Report to the Congress. Washington, D.C.

_____. (2008) *Rebuilding Iraq: DoD and State Department Have Improved Oversight and Coordination of Private Security Contractors in Iraq, but Further Actions Are Needed to Sustain Improvements*. Washington, D.C.

Guidry, Michael, and Guy Wills. (2004) "Future UAV Pilots: Are Contractors the Solution?" *Air Force Journal of Logistics* 28: 4–15.

Hanna, Mark. (1997) "Task Force XXI: The Army's Digital Experiment." Washington D.C.: National Defense University Institute for National Strategic Studies.

Hosek, James R., and Francisco Martorell. (2009) *Military Reenlistment and Deployment During the War on Terrorism*. Santa Monica, Calif.: RAND Corporation, RB-9468-OSD. As of April 19, 2010: http://www.rand.org/pubs/research_briefs/RB9468/

Hosek, James R., Michael G. Mattock, C. Christine Fair, Jennifer Kavanagh, Jennifer Sharp, and Mark Totten. (2004) *Attracting the Best: How the Military Competes for Information Technology Personnel*. Santa Monica, Calif.: RAND Corporation, MG-108. As of April 19, 2010: http://www.rand.org/pubs/monographs/MG108/

"Iraq to Seek Compensation for Contractor Incidents." (19 January 2010) *Washington Post*, 6.

Isenberg, David. (1997) *Soldiers of Fortune Ltd.: A Profile of Today's Private Sector Corporate Mercenary Firms*. Washington, D.C.: Center for Defense Information.

———. (2007) "A Government in Search of Cover: Private Military Companies in Iraq." In *From Mercenaries to Market*, Simon Chesterman and Chia Lenhardt, eds., pp. 82–93. New York: Oxford University Press.

———. (2009) *Shadow Force: Private Security Contractors in Iraq*. Westport, Conn.: Praeger Security International.

Ivanovich, David. (9 February 2008) "Contractor Deaths Up 17 Percent Across Iraq in 2007." *Houston Chronicle*.

Jansen, Jaime. (17 August 2006) "Federal Jury Reaches Partial Verdict in CIA Contractor Detainee Abuse Case." *JURIST Legal News and Research*.

Johnson, Michael. (2007) "Contractors on the Battlefield: Walking the Legal Combatant Tightrope." Maxwell Air Force Base, Ala.: Air Command Staff College.

Johnston, David, and John M. Broder. (14 November 2007) "FBI Says Guards Killed 14 Iraqis Without Cause." *New York Times*.

Joint Chiefs of Staff. (1995) JP 4-05, "Joint Doctrine for Mobilization and Training." Washington, D.C.

———. (1996) *Joint Vision 2010*. Washington, D.C.

Kerr, Graham. (2008) "Security in Iraq: The Private Security Perspective." *Journal of International Peace Operations* 3: 17–18.

Kidwell, Deborah. (2005) *Public War, Private Fight? The United States and Private Military Companies*. Fort Leavenworth, Kan.: Combat Studies Institute Occasional Paper.

Kinsey, Christopher. (2006) *Corporate Soldiers and International Security: The Rise of Private Military Companies*. New York, N.Y.: Routledge.

Klein, Alec. (24 August 2007) "For Security in Iraq, a Turn to British Know-How; with U.S. Contract up for Grabs, Congresswoman Requests Audit of Major Bidder." *Washington Post*, D01.

Lardner, Richard. (11 October 2007) "Six-Figure Bonuses Retain U.S. Commandos." *Washington Post*.

Leander, Anna. (2006) *Eroding State Authority? Private Military Companies and the Legitimate Use of Force*. Rome: Centro Militaire di Studi Strategici.

Lee, Matthew. (20 November 2008) "U.S. Contractors Lose Immunity in Iraq Security Deal." *Seattle Post-Intelligencer*.

Logan, Lara. (13 October 2007) "Interview with Erik Prince." *60 Minutes*.

Luban, Daniel. (19 September 2007) "Blackwater Pays Price for Iraqi Firefight." *Asia Times*.

Lynch, Tony, and A. J. Walsh. (2000) "The Good Mercenary?" *Journal of Political Philosophy* 8: 133–153.

McGrath, John J. (2006) *Boots on the Ground: Troop Density in Contingency Operations.* Global War on Terrorism Occasional Paper 16. Ft. Leavenworth, Kan.: Combat Studies Institute Press.

Merle, Renae. (5 December 2006) "Census Counts 100,000 Contractors in Iraq." *Washington Post.*

Milburn, John, and Stephen Manning. (3 December 2008) "U.S. Soldiers, Swayed by Bad Economy, Are Re-Enlisting." *Houston Chronicle.*

Miller, T. Christian. (4 July 2007) "Contractors Outnumber U.S. Troops in Iraq." *Virginian Pilot,* A9.

Montagne, Renee, and Dina Temple-Raston. (17 December 2007) "Iraqis See U.S. Contractors, Troops the Same." *National Public Radio.*

Nichols, Camille. (1996) "The Logistics Civil Augmentation Program." *Military Review* 76, March–April: 65–72.

National Defense University. (2008) "Privatized Military Operations Industry." Fort McNair, Washington D.C: Industrial College of the Armed Forces.

Nelson, Kim. (2000) "Contractors on the Battlefield: Force Multipliers or Force Dividers?" Maxwell Air Force Base, Ala.: Air Command and Staff College.

Office of Budget and Management. (2002) *The President's Management Agenda.* Washington, D.C.

O'Harrow, Robert. (30 January 2009) "State Department Cancels Iraq Contract with Blackwater." *Washington Post.*

O'Meara, Kelly. (4 Feb. 2002a) "DynCorp Disgrace." *Insight Magazine.*

———. (29 April 2002b) "Broken Wings." *Insight Magazine.*

Oppel, Richard A., and Michael R. Gordon. (11 October 2007) "U.S. Military and Iraqis Say They Are Shut Out of Inquiry." *New York Times.*

Orsini, Eric, and Gary Bublitz. (1999) "Contractors on the Battlefield: Risks on the Road Ahead?" *Army Logistician,* January–February.

Palmer, Herman T. (1999) "More Tooth, Less Tail: Contractors in Bosnia." *Army Logistician,* September–October, 6–9.

Pelton, Robert Young. (2007) *Licensed to Kill: Hired Guns in the War on Terror.* New York: Three Rivers Press.

Percy, Sarah. (2007) "Mercenaries: Strong Norm, Weak Law." *International Organization* 61: 367–397.

———. (2003) "This Gun's for Hire." *International Journal* 58: 721–736.

Petersohn, Ulrich. (2007) "Outsourcing the Big Stick—The Consequences of Using Private Military Companies." Weatherhead Center Working Paper. Cambridge.

Phinney, David. (7 June 2005) "Marines Jail Contractors in Iraq: Tension and Confusion Grow Amid the 'Fog of War.'" *CorpWatch.*

Priest, Dana. (April 6, 2004) "Private Guards Repel Attack on U.S. Headquarters." *Washington Post.*

"Protocol Additional to the Geneva Conventions of 12 August 1949, and Relating to the Protection of Victims of International Armed Conflicts (Protocol 1)." (Adopted 8 June 1977; Entered into force: 7 December 1979).

Scahill, Jeremy. (2007) *Blackwater: The Rise of the World's Most Powerful Mercenary Army.* New York: Nation Books.

Schakowsky, Congresswoman Jan. (6 August 2007) "Schakowsky Uncovers 1,001 Contractor Deaths in Iraq." Press release.

Schaller, Christian. (2007) "Private Security and Military Companies Under the International Law of Armed Conflict." In *Private Military and Security Companies*, Gerhard Kuemmel and Thomas Jaeger, eds., pp. 345–360. Wiesbaden: VS Verlag.

———. (2005) "Private Sicherheitsfirmen- und Militaerfirmen in Bewaffneten Konflikten." SWP Studie S24. Berlin: Stiftung Wissenschaft und Politik.

Schmitt, Michael. (2005) "Humanitarian Law and Direct Participation in Hostilities by Private Contractors or Civilian Employees." *Chicago Journal of International Law* 5: 11–46.

Schreier, Fred, and Marina Caparini. (2005) "Privatising Security: Law, Practice and Governance of Private Military and Security Companies." Geneva: Geneva Centre for the Democratic Control of Armed Forces Occasional Paper.

Schumacher, Gerald. (2006) *A Bloody Business: America's War Zone Contractors and the Occupation of Iraq.* St. Paul, Minn.: Zenith Press.

Shearer, David. (1998) "Private Armies and Military Intervention." New York: Oxford University Press for the International Institute for Strategic Studies.

Silverstein, Ken, and Daniel Burton-Rose. (2000) *Private Warriors.* New York: Verso.

Singer, Peter. (2003) *Corporate Warriors: The Rise of the Privatized Military Industry.* Ithaca, N.Y.: Cornell University Press.

———. (2004) "Should Humanitarians Use Private Military Services?" *Humanitarian Affairs Review. Summer.*

———. (2007) "Can't Win with 'Em, Can't Go to War Without 'Em: Private Military Contractors and Counterinsurgency." Washington, D.C.: The Brookings Institution.

Sizemore, Bill, and Joanne Kimberlin. (26 July 2006) "Blackwater: When Things Go Wrong." *Virginian-Pilot.*

Smith, Eugene. (Winter 2003) "The New Condottieri and US Policy: The Privatization of Conflict and Its Implications." *Parameters,* 104–119.

Spearin, Christopher. (Winter 2006) "Special Operations Forces a Strategic Resource: Public and Private Divides." *Parameters,* 58–70.

Special Inspector General for Iraq Reconstruction. (2005) *Audit Report: Compliance with the Contract No. W911s0-04-C-0003 Awarded Aegis Defense Service Limited.* Washington, D.C.

Stoeber, Jan. (2007) "Contracting in the Fog of War. Private Security Providers in Iraq: A Principal-Agent Analysis." In *Private Military and Security Companies*, Thomas Jaeger and Gerhard Kuemmel, eds., pp. 121–134. Wiesbaden: VS Verlag.

Stout, David. (4 October 2007) "House Bill Would Allow Prosecution of Contractors." *New York Times.*

Tanielian, Terri, and Lisa H. Jaycox, eds. (2008) *Invisible Wounds of War: Psychological and Cognitive Injuries, Their Consequences, and Services to Assist Recovery.* Santa Monica, Calif.: RAND Corporation, MG-720-CCF. As of April 13, 2010: http://www.rand.org/pubs/monographs/MG720/

Thomson, Janice. (1994) *Mercenaries, Pirates, & Sovereigns.* Princeton: Princeton University Press.

Traynor, Ian. (10 December 2003) "The Privatisation of War." *The Guardian.*

Urey, Ronda. (2005) "Civilian Contractors on the Battlefield." Carlisle Barracks, Pa.: U.S. Army War College.

"U.S. Appeals Ruling in Blackwater Case." (30 January 2010) *Washington Post*, 16.

Vainshtein, Robert. (January 2007) "UCMJ v. MEJA: Two Options For Regulating Contractors." *Journal of International Peace Operations* 2(4): 3.

Vines, Alex. (2002) "Gurkhas and the Private Security Business in Africa." In *Peace, Profit or Plunder*, Jakkie Cilliers and Peggy Mason, eds., pp. 123–140. Pretoria: Institute for Security Studies.

Westervelt, Eric. (13 June 2005). "Profile: Confusion in Iraq over Alleged Incident Between Marines and Private Contractors." *National Public Radio Morning Edition*.

Williams, Timothy. (2 January 2010) "Iraqis Angered As Blackwater Charges Are Dropped." *New York Times*, A4.

Witte, Griff. (8 September 2005) "Private Security Contractors Head to Gulf." *Washington Post*, A14.

Wolfendale, Jessica. (2008) "The Military and the Community: Comparing National Military Forces and Private Military Companies." In *Private Military and Security Companies*, Andrew Alexandra, Deane-Peter Baker, and Marina Caparini, eds., pp. 217–234. London: Routledge.

Wynn, James. (25 June 2004) *Statement Before the United States House, Committee on Armed Services*. Washington, D.C.

Zamparelli, Steven. (1999) "Contractors on the Battlefield: What Have We Signed up For?" *Air Force Journal of Logistics* 23: 11–19.

Zarate, Juan Carlos. (1998) "The Emergence of a New Dog of War: Private International Security Companies, International Law, and New World Disorder." *Stanford Journal of International Law* 34: 75–162.